THOMAS HARDY AND THE DEATH OF EMMA

WHAT HIS WRITINGS REVEAL

Andrew Norman

WHITE OWL
AN IMPRINT OF PEN & SWORD BOOKS LTD.
YORKSHIRE – PHILADELPHIA

First published in Great Britain in 2024 by
PEN AND SWORD WHITE OWL
An imprint of
Pen & Sword Books Ltd
Yorkshire – Philadelphia

ISBN 978 1 39905 117 0

A CIP catalogue record for this book is available from the British Library.

Typeset in Times New Roman 10.5/13 by
SJmagic DESIGN SERVICES, India.
Printed and bound in the UK by CPI Group (UK) Ltd, Croydon, CR0 4YY.

Pen & Sword Books Limited incorporates the imprints of Atlas, Archaeology, Aviation, Discovery, Family History, Fiction, History, Maritime, Military, Military Classics, Politics, Select, Transport, True Crime, Air World, Frontline Publishing, Leo Cooper, Remember When, Seaforth Publishing, The Praetorian Press, Wharncliffe Local History, Wharncliffe Transport, Wharncliffe True Crime, White Owl and After the Battle.

For a complete list of Pen & Sword titles please contact

PEN & SWORD BOOKS LIMITED
George House, Units 12 & 13, Beevor Street, Off Pontefract Road,
Barnsley, South Yorkshire, S71 1HN, England
E-mail: enquiries@pen-and-sword.co.uk
Website: www.pen-and-sword.co.uk

or

PEN AND SWORD BOOKS
1950 Lawrence Rd, Havertown, PA 19083, USA
E-mail: uspen-and-sword@casematepublishers.com
Website: www.penandswordbooks.com

MIX
Paper | Supporting responsible forestry
FSC www.fsc.org
FSC® C013604

THOMAS HARDY AND THE DEATH OF EMMA

In memory of my beloved late wife
(Alison) Rachel Norman
1945–2022

Lux Vitae Meae

To beloved Penny

Qui Semper Est in Corde Meo
Et in Cogitationibus Meis

Beeny Cliff

O the opal and the sapphire of that wandering western sea,
And the woman riding high above with bright hair flapping free –
The woman whom I loved so, and who loyally loved me.

– Still in all its chasmal beauty bulks old Beeny to the sky,
And shall she and I not go there once again now March is nigh,
And the sweet things said in that March say anew there by and by?

What if still in chasmal beauty looms that wild weird western shore,
The woman now is – elsewhere – whom the ambling pony bore,
And nor knows nor cares for Beeny, and will laugh there nevermore.

by Thomas Hardy (Verses I,IV,V)

Author's note

In *Literature and Modern Time*, published by Springer Nature, Switzerland in 2020, Trish Ferguson, Professor of English Literature at Liverpool Hope University, UK, contributed a chapter entitled '"Time's Renewal": Death and Immortality in Thomas Hardy's "Emma Poems".' In the chapter, Trish quoted Tess Durbeyfield who, in Hardy's novel *Tess of the D'Urbervilles*, asked her husband Angel Clare, 'Do you think we shall meet again after we are dead?' To this, there was no reply. This was a question that obsessed Hardy throughout his life, as will be seen.

Contents

About the Author

Andrew Norman was born in Newbury, Berkshire, UK in 1943. Having been educated at Thornhill High School, Gwelo, Southern Rhodesia (now Zimbabwe), Midsomer Norton Grammar School, and St Edmund Hall, Oxford, he qualified in medicine at the Radcliffe Infirmary. He has two children Bridget and Thomas, by his first wife.

From 1972-83, Andrew worked as a general practitioner in Poole, Dorset, before a spinal injury cut short his medical career. He is now an established writer whose published works include biographies of Charles Darwin, Winston Churchill, Thomas Hardy, T. E. Lawrence, Adolf Hitler, Agatha Christie, Enid Blyton, Beatrix Potter, Marilyn Monroe, and Sir Arthur Conan Doyle. Andrew married his second wife Rachel, in 2005.

Author's website: https://www.andrew-norman.co.uk

Acknowledgements

Dorset History Centre; Dorset Museum; Registration Services, Dorset Council; The National Trust, Max Gate, Dorchester; The Thomas Hardy Society; Dr Tracy Hayes.

Author's Note

In many of his poems, the great Dorset poet and novelist Thomas Hardy referred to a certain romantic courtship, a marriage which became progressively more problematical, and finally to a bereavement in which a man loses his wife. So, who was Hardy writing about? The clue is in his early poems, where the names of several locations in North Cornwall are mentioned, this being the very same place which featured in Hardy's courtship of Emma Gifford, who was to become his first wife. In other words, Hardy was writing about his own experience of love, marriage, and loss.

The poems raise certain questions. Given that Hardy and Emma gradually drifted apart so that in the end they lived mainly separate lives, albeit under the same roof, why was he so grief-stricken when she died, bearing in mind that their marriage was so unsatisfactory?

How did Hardy cope as he passed through the various stages of grief, which he articulated so poignantly and expressively in his poems? These stages are recognized today, thanks to the work of Swiss-US psychiatrist, Elisabeth Kübler-Ross, and US expert on grieving and loss, David Kessler.

Finally, how did Hardy survive and come out the other side, and can his experience be a guide to others who find themselves alone and bereft after losing their partner?

Introduction

It is impossible to understand the poetry of Thomas Hardy without first knowing the context in which the poems were written, and this is especially true of the poems that he wrote after the death of his wife Emma, which is the subject of this narrative. In his poetry, like nowhere else, Hardy expressed his grief over the loss of Emma and within these poems are clues to his deepest thoughts and feelings. Here, Hardy's poems are reappraised in the light of modern psychology and, in particular, in the light of the groundbreaking work of Elisabeth Kübler-Ross.

Hardy was an incurable romantic even as a boy and he was forever falling in love, even though the female objects of his desire were often completely unaware of his amorous feelings towards them.

Hardy was dazzled by the beauty of his wife-to-be, Emma, and when he met her, it was love at first sight; in his words, 'magic'! However, this joyous state of affairs did not last, and in his poems, he alluded to the fact that his marriage to her was not a happy one. This much is borne out by the fact that in the later years they became estranged from one another and lived virtually separate lives at their home Max Gate, in Dorchester. This disunity is reflected in the poems.

Finally, it is no coincidence that although Hardy does not mention Emma by name in the several dozen poems that he wrote after her tragic and untimely death, he clearly alluded to her. When Emma suddenly died, Hardy was filled with grief and remorse. Yet in his poems, he reflected not only upon the later years of their marriage, when they became more and more estranged from each other, and upon her death and its aftermath, but also upon their first meeting and the happy and joyous days of their courtship.

Hardy's poems give a unique insight into his profoundest feelings for Emma, both on meeting her, during their courtship and marriage, and after her tragic death.

The relationship between Hardy and Emma in the later years of her life has been the subject of much controversy but, suffice it to say, that they grew further and further apart as a couple. Did Emma's personality change as the years progressed, or was it simply that Hardy had not recognized her for what she was when they first met and was, instead, carried away by her undoubted physical beauty? Or was it that Hardy himself had changed, and consequently fallen out of love with her?

Whatever the answer, the fact remains that Hardy was utterly grief-stricken by the loss of Emma, and he responded by going through all the classical phases of grief which are well known to psychologists and bereavement counsellors today.

As a bereaved person myself, I feel I am in an especially advantageous position to empathize with Hardy, who like me, lost the precious love of his life and the precious light of his life. But this is not all that I have in common with the great Dorset man-of-letters. My 'Norman' ancestors, for example, came from Fordington which is only a short distance from Higher Bockhampton where Hardy was born and spent his formative years. Furthermore, the Vicar of Fordington, the Reverend Henry Moule, baptized the infant Norman children back in the 19th century at Fordington's Parish Church of Saint George, and it was Moule's son Horace, of Cambridge University, who became Hardy's dearest friend.

In his grief, what comfort did Hardy have, following the death of his beloved Emma? Not in religion, surely, as he was a confirmed atheist. Not for him the prospect of resurrection and everlasting life, and of being reunited with Emma, or if he did entertain such hopes, he had little expectation of them being fulfilled. So how *did* Hardy manage to survive, which fortunately for mankind and for all lovers of poetry and literature, he did? And in examining Hardy's life, are there lessons to be learnt which might help others who find themselves in a similar position to summon up the strength to put one foot in front of the other once more, in short, to soldier on.

I firmly believe that only a bereaved person such as myself who has lost his beloved partner and soulmate, is in a position to comprehend the full significance of Hardy's 'Emma Poems'.

Did Hardy survive this cataclysmic event unscathed, or was he permanently scarred by it? In any event, what were his coping mechanisms and how effective were they?

Chapter 1

Thomas Hardy: The First Seven Decades

1. A Timeline of Hardy's Life, up to the Death of Emma

Thomas Hardy was born on 2 June 1840 at Higher Bockhampton, Dorset, in a five-roomed thatched dwelling standing on the edge of the heath and built by his great-grandfather John in 1801.

He was the eldest child of his namesake Thomas Hardy (born on 18 November 1811), a mason and builder employing 6 men from Higher Bockhampton near Dorchester, Dorset's county town, and his wife Jemima (née Hand, born on 21 September 1813), formerly a domestic servant from Melbury Osmond in north Dorset. Hardy's younger siblings were Mary (born on 23 December 1841), Henry (born on 1 July 1851), and Catherine ('Kate', born on 2 September 1856). 'Catherine' is sometimes spelt 'Katharine', for instance on her tombstone.[1]

Hardy's mother Jemima possessed a modest library of books. She was keen for her children to be educated and she paid for their lessons in honey produced from her own beehives. It was undoubtedly through her that Hardy derived his passion for literature. Meanwhile, as a child Hardy was taught to play the violin by his father, who played the bass viol.

From 1848, when he was 8-years-old, until 1856, Hardy attended the Bockhampton National School, and subsequently a day school in Dorchester whose headmaster was scholar and teacher of Latin, Isaac Last.

In 1856, when he was aged 16, Hardy made a painting of his pet rabbit 'Juno I'. He was always fond of animals and throughout his life cared deeply about their welfare and about how they were treated.

It was clear that Hardy, from a young age, had an extraordinary talent. For example, again at the age of 16 he composed a poem about his home entitled *Domicilium* (published, but only in pamphlet form, in 1916). It begins as follows:

> I
> It faces west and round the back and sides
> High beeches, bending, hang a veil of boughs,
> And sweep against the roof. Wild honeysucks

> Climb on the walls, and seem to sprout a wish
> (If we may fancy wish of trees and plants)
> To overtop the apple trees hard by.

The poem reveals how Hardy used his imagination, in this instance to think of flora as well as fauna, as having sentient feelings.

Publisher and author Newman Flower (1879-1964)'s, family home was at West Stafford, less than 2 miles from Hardy's home at Max Gate. It was 'before the First World War' (1914-1918), he said, that he first met Hardy, and the two men became firm friends.[2] Flower described how he:

> 'was out walking one day with Hardy; we were going to Came, the small village nearby of which his old friend, William Barnes, the Dorset poet, had been rector, and in the churchyard of which he lies now. We talked about Barnes a great deal.' Hardy became a friend of Barnes, and no doubt, became familiar with his literary works.

William Barnes (1801–1886) was a polymath; a writer, poet, philologist, priest, mathematician, engraving artist, and inventor. 'He wrote over eight-hundred poems, some in Dorset dialect, and much other work, including a comprehensive English grammar quoting from more than 70 different languages.'[3]

'The great scholar who, living in a Dorset village, was one of the finest Latin and Oriental language authorities of his age. Quite apart from the fact that he is regarded as the greatest of the country poets, he wrote books of fine scholarship: *A Philological Grammar* [1854], which formed a comparison of more than sixty languages; An *Anglo-Saxon Delectus* [Elementary Reader, 1849], and other works. Hardy and Barnes were close friends ....'[4] Furthermore, the fact that Hardy's library contained several of Barnes's books is surely no coincidence!

Hardy acquired a vocabulary that was second to none. He therefore had more tools at his disposal when it came to selecting the appropriate word or phrase than virtually any other writer before or since to convey his meaning.

As a young man, Hardy taught at Sunday School, and even considered becoming a vicar.

From 1856 to 1860 Hardy was employed as architectural apprentice to architect John Hicks of Dorchester, and he later became Hicks's assistant. Meanwhile, he studied Latin and Greek in his spare time.

Hardy's sisters trained at the Diocesan Training College in Salisbury, Wiltshire, where Mary enrolled in 1860 and Kate in 1877. Mary subsequently became (Head) Mistress of Dorchester's National School for Girls, in Bell Street (established in 1816 for 315 children), where Kate subsequently joined her as Assistant Mistress. As for Hardy's brother Henry, he followed in his father Thomas's footsteps, became a builder, and subsequently inherited the family business.

For a period of 10 years, from 1860 to 1870, Hardy made pencil sketches and notes in his architectural notebook about renovations to churches, public buildings, and private homes. In 1862, when he was aged 22, Hardy moved to London to pursue a career in architecture. Here, architect, church designer and restorer Arthur Blomfield employed him as a draughtsman. In 1867, Hardy returned to Dorset, where he resumed working for Hicks on church restoration.

In 1868, Hardy completed his first novel, *The Poor Man and the Lady*, but it was rejected by the publisher.

In 1869, Hardy found employment with architect George R. Crickmay of Weymouth, Dorset and was again engaged in what was euphemistically described as 'church restoration' – a process which involved the destruction of many important historical artefacts within the buildings in question.

In 1870, whilst visiting St Juliot in North Cornwall in a professional capacity, Hardy met 29-year-old Emma Lavinia Gifford, who was 5 months his junior. The date was 7 March and the journey entailed catching the train from Dorchester North Station, changing trains at Exeter St David's, changing again for Launceston, and finally taking a pony and trap for the final eighteen miles to St Juliot.

This experience was without doubt the most stupendously exhilarating of Hardy's life. He was, to use a modern phrase, 'blown away' by Emma's beauty. But sadly, because of the distance involved – it is 120 miles from Weymouth to St Juliot, the pair were able to meet only infrequently thereafter.

A spate of novels quickly followed: *Desperate Remedies* (1871); *Under the Greenwood Tree* (1872); *A Pair of Blue Eyes* (1873).

On 17 September 1874, Hardy married Emma and the couple set up home in Surbiton, London. (The marriage was to be childless.) In 1875 the Hardys returned to Dorset where, in the coastal resort of Swanage, Hardy completed *The Hand of Ethelberta* (published in 1876).

The Return of the Native was published in 1878, when the Hardys were living at Riverside Villa, Sturminster Newton, Dorset. In that same year, the Hardys returned to London (Tooting). Three more novels followed in successive years: *The Trumpet-Major* (1880); *A Laodicean* (1881); *Two on a Tower* (1882).

In 1885 the Hardys relocated to Max Gate, on the outskirts of Dorchester, a house designed by Hardy and built by his brother Henry. Here they remained for the rest of their lives, and here Hardy wrote *The Mayor of Casterbridge* (1886); *The Woodlanders* (1887); *Wessex Tales* (1888); *A Group of Noble Dames* (1891); *Tess of the D'Urbervilles* (1891).

However, during much of the 27 years spent together at Max Gate, far from enjoying marital harmony and bliss, Hardy and Emma lived largely separate lives, for reasons which will be discussed shortly.

On 20 July 1892, Hardy's father Thomas died.

There followed three more novels: *Life's Little Ironies* (1894); *Jude the Obscure* (1895); *The Well-Beloved* (1897). And then came an outpouring of poetry, published as: *Wessex Poems and Other Verses* (1898); *Poems of the Past and the Present* (1901). Also, Part I of *The Dynasts* (1904) an epic-drama in verse about Napoleon. On 3 April 1904, Hardy's mother Jemima died.

In 1905, Hardy met Florence Emily Dugdale, a schoolteacher, journalist, and writer of children's stories. She subsequently made prolonged visits to Max Gate, where she befriended Emma and assisted Hardy with his writing and correspondence.

Meanwhile the outpouring of poetry continued unabated, with Part II of *The Dynasts* (1906); Part III of *The Dynasts* (1908); and another collection of poems *Time's Laughingstocks and Other Verses* (1909).

In 1910 Hardy was awarded the Order of Merit, an order founded in 1902 for distinguished achievement, with membership limited to twenty-four persons.[5] He had previously declined the offer of a knighthood.

On 27 November 1912, Emma died. 'This triggered the writing of Hardy's finest love-lyrics about their early time in Cornwall.'[6]

2. Life Before Emma: How Hardy Pondered Over Life, Love, and Loss

In 1866, four years before he first met his wife-to-be Emma, when he was in his 26th year, Hardy composed the poem *She to Him* (published in 1898), in which he acknowledged that ageing and death were inevitable:

When you shall see me lined by tool of Time,
My lauded beauties carried off from me,
My eyes no longer stars as in their prime,
My name forgot of Maiden Fair and Free;

When in your being heart concedes to mind,
And judgment, though you scarce its process know,
Recalls the excellencies I once enshrined,
And you are irked that they have withered so:

Remembering that with me lies not the blame,
That Sportsman Time but rears his brood to kill,
Knowing me in my soul the very same -
One who would die to spare you touch of ill! -
Will you not grant to old affection's claim
The hand of friendship down Life's sunless hill?

For one so young, this indicates an incredible maturity on Hardy's part, not to say solemnity or even morbidness!

In his poem *Neutral Tones* (composed in 1867, and published in 1898), Hardy revealed that he was aware that love can deceive.

> We stood by a pond that winter day,
> And the sun was white, as though chidden of God,
> And a few leaves lay on the starving sod;
> – They had fallen from an ash, and were gray.
>
> Your eyes on me were as eyes that rove
> Over tedious riddles of years ago;
> And some words played between us to-and-fro
> On which lost the more by our love.
>
> The smile on your mouth was the deadest thing
> Alive enough to have strength to die;
> And a grin of bitterness swept thereby
> Like an ominous bird a-wing....
>
> Since then, keen lessons that love deceives,
> And wrings with wrong, have shaped to me
> Your face, and the God curst sun, and a tree,
> And a pond edged with grayish leaves.

Chidden: scolded or rebuked.[1]

Once again, Hardy displayed a maturity beyond his years, but of course, at this relatively young age he could not have known what was in store for him personally!

3. Early Disappointments in Love

From his poem *Revulsion* (composed in 1866 when he was in his 26th year and published in 1898), it appears that Hardy had already been disappointed in love and felt extremely bitter about it:

> Though I waste watches framing words to fetter
> Some spirit to mine own in clasp and kiss,
> Out of the night there looms a sense 'twere better
> To fail obtaining whom one fails to miss.

For winning love we win the risk of losing,
And losing love is as one's life were riven;
It cuts like contumely and keen ill-using
To cede what was superfluously given.

Let me then feel no more the fateful thrilling
That devastates the love-worn wooer's frame,
The hot ado of fevered hopes, the chilling
That agonizes disappointed aim!
So may I live no junctive law fulfilling,
And my heart's table bear no woman's name.

But despite this advice to himself, Hardy did not entirely give up in his pursuit of love, as will be seen!

4. When Hardy Met Emma (7 March 1870)

In his poem '*When I Set Out for Lyonnesse*' (composed in 1870, and published in 1914), Hardy described his joy at meeting Emma Lavinia Gifford for the first time in that same year at St Juliot in Cornwall and being bowled over by her beauty. Emma was the sister of Helen Catherine (née Gifford), whose husband the Reverend Caddell Holder was Rector of St Julitta's Church, St Juliot, dedicated to St Julitta, a male Celtic saint of the fifth century.

It so happened that when Hardy first arrived on the scene, in his aforementioned capacity as assistant architect to George Crickmay of Weymouth, the Reverend Holder was suffering from an attack of gout. Helen was attending her husband and it was therefore Emma, who was currently residing with the couple, who received the visitor. As for the church, it had, 'for many years been in a ruinous condition, and 'no service' had 'been held in it for more than two years'.[1] Said Emma:

> 'The tower went on cracking from year to year and the bells remained in little North Transept, their mouths open upward. The carved bench-ends rotted more and more, the ivy hung gaily from the roof-timbers and the birds and the bats had a good time up there unmolested; no one seemed to care.'[2]

The arrival of architect Hardy was therefore a matter of great interest and excitement in the parish, for now, at last, the long-awaited plans for the 'restoration' of the church could be put into operation: restoration being, in Hardy's view, a euphemism for destruction, in which he was an unwilling participant.

The Church of St Julitta was 'restored' – in what, in Hardy's opinion, was largely an act of architectural vandalism - between 1870 and 1872 and reopened on 25 April 1872. This involved the demolition and rebuilding of the tower, north aisle, and transept. In the event, and much to Hardy's dismay, much of the mediaeval portions of the church were destroyed during its so-called 'restoration', something which Hardy always regretted. However, he did manage to record some of its lost features, in several sketches that he made. They included the bench ends and the north door. Later in life, Hardy campaigned to protect such mediaeval features in other churches.

The evening of Hardy's arrival, said Emma, was 'lovely ... after a wild winter'. She also recalled that Hardy 'had a beard' and was wearing 'a rather shabby great coat'. A blue paper protruded from his pocket which proved to be, not a plan of the church, but the manuscript of a poem he had written. Emma stated that on his first visit to the church, 'the architect [Hardy] ... stayed a few days rather longer than first intended'.[3]

Two days after his arrival, Hardy, accompanied by Emma and her sister Helen, visited Boscastle (2 miles west of St Julitta's Rectory); Tintagel (5 miles south-west of St Julitta's Rectory and the legendary birthplace of the legendary King Arthur), and the quarries of Penpethy to seek slate for the roofing of the church. Next day, Hardy and Emma walked, unchaperoned, on the cliff tops. She loved the 'beautiful sea-coast, [and] the wild Atlantic Ocean rolling in, with its magnificent waves and spray', she said, and declared that she and Hardy could scarcely have had a more romantic meeting.[4]

On the fourth day Hardy returned home. He later summed up just how deeply his own romantic instincts had been aroused by his meeting with Emma in a poem entitled '*When I Set Out for Lyonnesse*', and in particular, in the poem's final verse:

When I set out for Lyonnesse,
  A hundred miles away,
  The rime was on the spray,
And starlight lit my lonesomeness
When I set out for Lyonnesse
  A hundred miles away.

What would bechance at Lyonnesse
  While I should sojourn there
  No prophet durst declare,
Nor did the wisest wizard guess
What would bechance at Lyonnesse
  While I should sojourn there.

When I came back from Lyonnesse
  With magic in my eyes,
  All marked with mute surmise
My radiance rare and fathomless,
When I came back from Lyonnesse
  With magic in my eyes!

Lyonesse: a kingdom which, according to legend, consisted of a long strand of land stretching from Land's End at the south-western tip of Cornwall, England, to what are now known as the Isles of Scilly in the Celtic Sea portion of the Atlantic Ocean. Lyonesse was considered lost after being swallowed by the ocean in a single night.[5]

Hardy, always a romantic by nature, had evidently found the woman of his dreams. From then on, he returned to St Juliot whenever time allowed, which was every few months, and took the opportunity to visit other local beauty spots with Emma including the beautiful Valency Valley, through which the Valency River flows.

On one of his occasional visits to Cornwall, after he and Emma had enjoyed a shared picnic together, Hardy sketched her as she attempted to retrieve a drinking glass that she had accidentally dropped into a stream. Hardy commemorated this event in his poem *Under the Waterfall*.

5. More About Emma

Emma was born on 24 November 1840 at 10 York Street, Plymouth, Devonshire. She was the younger daughter of solicitor John Attersoll Gifford and his wife Emma (née Farman). Emma was 5 months younger than Hardy.

In June 1860, the Gifford family relocated from Plymouth to Bodmin in Cornwall. Here, Emma's elder sister Helen obtained a post, first as a governess (in which capacity she was succeeded, for a brief period, by Emma), and then as companion to an elderly lady at Tintagel on the coast. There, Helen met her husband-to-be, the Reverend Caddell Holder, MA Oxon, rector of St Juliot, the repair of whose church was the objective of Hardy's visit.

The Reverend Holder was born on the Caribbean Island of Barbados, where his father was a judge, and educated at Trinity College, Oxford. When he married Helen, on 10 September 1868 at Bodmin parish church, he was aged 67, and she only 31. (This was Holder's second marriage; his first wife Ann having died three years previously.) When Holder took his new wife back to his home, Emma accompanied them.

At St Julitta's Rectory, Emma helped her sister with 'house affairs' and also paid visits to the parish folk (that is, her brother-in-law's parishioners).[1] Her spare time was spent riding her pony 'Fanny', painting in watercolour, and sketching and gathering wild flowers. On Sundays she played the harmonium and 'conducted the church music'.[2] Emma was clearly a very gifted young lady.

During Hardy and Emma's honeymoon in France, following their wedding on 17 September 1874, Emma kept a diary in which she sketched, and wrote about her experiences.

6. Marital Discord

Hardy's poem *We Sat at the Window* (published in 1917) was composed in Bournemouth, on the south coast of Hampshire (now Dorset) on St Swithin's Day, 15 July 1875. This was the tenth month following his marriage to Emma. In the poem, Hardy alluded to the fact that already, there were serious problems in regard to their relationship. After all, who else could he have been referring to in the poem?

> We sat at the window looking out,
> And the rain came down like silken strings
> That Swithin's day. Each gutter and spout
> Babbled unchecked in the busy way
> Of witless things:
> Nothing to read, nothing to see
> Seemed in that room for her and me
> On Swithin's day.
>
> We were irked by the scene, by our own selves; yes,
> For I did not know, nor did she infer
> How much there was to read and guess
> By her in me, and to see and crown
> By me in her.
> Wasted were two souls in their prime,
> And great was the waste, that July time
> When the rain came down.

Could it really be that Hardy discovered that he and Emma were incompatible as a married couple so soon after their wedding? And did this include sexual incompatibility. And if so, was this at the root of the problem?

In his poem *The Spell of the Rose* (published in 1914), Hardy described how his marriage to Emma subsequently became an unbearable nightmare (She, undoubtedly, felt the same way!):

III
'Some heart-bane moved our souls to sever …

'And misconceits raised horrid shows,
And agonies came thereof.'

And he spoke of:

IV
'… divisions dire and wry,
And long-drawn days of blight'

Those who are unfamiliar with Hardy's life, and the full details of his marriage to Emma, and who are ignorant of the context in which his poems were composed, may not understand just how much of their relationship is revealed in his poetry. An excellent example of this is in his poem *To a Sea-Cliff* (published in 1925) composed following a visit by Emma and himself to Durlston Head in the Isle of Purbeck, south Dorset. In the poem, Hardy admitted the brutal truth, that his marriage to Emma had been a disastrous failure, the final line of the poem being the most poignant and shocking.

Lend me an ear
While I read you here
A page from your history,
Old cliff — not known
To your solid stone,
Yet yours inseparably.

Near to your crown
There once sat down
A silent listless pair;
And the sunset ended,
And dark descended,
And still the twain sat there.

Past your jutting head
Then a line-ship sped,
Lit brightly as a city;

And she sobbed: 'There goes
A man who knows
I am his, beyond God's pity!'

He slid apart
Who had thought her heart
His own, and not aboard
A bark, sea-bound ....
That night they found
Between them lay a sword.

'Line-ship': a naval warship: ship of the line.

The final couplet of this poem implies that Hardy's marriage to Emma was never consummated, which would explain why the couple never had children.

It is unlikely that Hardy was impotent, the indications being that he fathered at least one illegitimate child, as will be seen. Did Hardy see himself as being impotent? Certainly not. In his last will and testament, made in August 1922 when he was eighty-two years of age, he made provision for 'the first child of mine who shall attain the age of twenty-one years'![1] By this time his second wife Florence was aged forty-three!

In Hardy's poem *A Poor Man and a Lady* (published in 1925), he echoed his belief that because of his lower station in life, he was not worthy to marry Emma, a belief which her family shared and made only too clear to him. Emma's father, for example, described Hardy as 'a low-born churl'.[2]

Churl: a rude and mean-spirited person.[3]

Furthermore, in the poem, Hardy implied that Emma did not regard herself as truly married to him, even though they had in fact been formally and officially married. Faced with this, the 'inferior' man in the poem finally parts from the 'superior woman', who goes on to marry somebody else who she considers to be more worthy and deserving. In real life, Hardy parted from Emma, but only in spirit as, despite their marital difficulties, they continued to live separate lives together at Max Gate under the same roof, but nevertheless attended the occasional social function which they hosted together. This was presumably for appearances sake:

I
We knew it was not a valid thing,
And only sanct in the sight of God
(To use your phrase), as with fervent nod
You swore your assent when I placed the ring
On your pale slim hand. Our whispering
Was soft as the fan of a turtledove

That round our heads might have seemed to wing;
So solemn were we; so sincere our love.

II
We could do no better; and thus it stood
Through a time of timorous secret bliss,
Till we were divided, and never a kiss
Of mine could touch you, or likelihood
Illumed our sky that we might, or should
Be each to each in the world's wide eye
What we were unviewed; and our vows make good
In the presence of parents and standers by.

V
We met in a Mayfair church, alone:
(The request was mine, which you yielded to).
'But we were not married at all!' urged you:
'Why, of course we were!' I said. Your tone,
I noted, was world-wise. You went on:
'Twas sweet while it lasted. But you well know
That law is law. He'll be, anon,
My husband *really*. You, Dear, weren't so.'

VI
'I wished — but to learn if — 'faltered I,
And stopped. 'But I'll sting you not. Farewell!'
And we parted. — Do you recall the bell
That tolled by chance as we said good-bye? …
I saw you no more. The track of a high,
Sweet, liberal lady you've doubtless trod.
— All's past! No heart was burst thereby,
And no one knew, unless it was God.

Sanct: sanctified, i.e. declared holy.[4]

Said Flower:

> 'For many years Hardy endured the hurt of domestic discord without a word of reproach. He drew more closely into himself. He spent his days in the solitude of his room.
>
> 'He returned on one occasion from a walk to discover that a young relative – a visitor - had been sent away during his absence,

> for no reason whatever. The peak of temperament aroused him at last to anger. He resolved to live his future life in his study. He consulted a builder as to the best way of building a stairway to his study from the garden so that he should not have to go the house to reach his room on any occasion. He would have all his meals in this room. He would live there. In the event, the stairway was never built.

In his poem *Song to Aurore* (published in 1928), Hardy revealed that so traumatized was he by his marital experience that he had come to believe that he could never love again.

We'll not begin again to love,
It only leads to pain;
The fire we now are master of
Has seared us not in vain.
Any new step of yours I'm fain
To hear of from afar,
And even in such may find a gain
While lodged not where you are.

No: that must not be done anew
Which has been done before;
I scarce could bear to seek, or view,
Or clasp you any more!
Life is a labour, death is sore,
And lonely living wrings;
But go your courses, Sweet Aurore,
Kisses are caresome things!

Aurora: in Roman mythology, the goddess of the dawn.[5]

Again, those who question whether Hardy was referring to himself and Emma in this poem should ask themselves, if not, then *who was* he referring to?

However, in his poem *Circus-Rider to Ringmaster* (published in 1925), Hardy indicated that yes, there *was a time* when he and Emma *had* loved one another:

IV
Shape the kiss you'd briskly blow up to me
        While our love was warm,
And my cheek unstained by tears,
        As in these last years!

7. A Visit from the Prince of Wales: Dorchester Honours Hardy

In 1910, the newly crowned King George V included Hardy in the birthday honours list. Having already turned down a knighthood, Hardy accepted the Order of Merit. He considered this award to be more appropriate because it was awarded for exceptional service 'towards the advancement of Arts, Learning, Literature, and Science'. On 19 July, the month after his 70th birthday, wrote Florence, Hardy travelled to Marlborough House, St James's, City of Westminster, London, where the King, 'received him pleasantly' for the investiture.[1]

On 16 November 1910, Hardy was made an Honorary Freeman of the Borough of Dorchester, the highest honour the council could bestow. His 'Freedom Scroll' was presented in a gilt casket and was given 'in recognition of his brilliant services to English Literature'. This particular honour, wrote Florence:

> 'appealed to his sentiment more perhaps than did many of those recognitions of his literary achievements that had come from the uttermost parts of the earth at a much earlier time.'[2]

Chapter 2

The Death of Emma (27 November 1912)

In *The Later Years of Thomas Hardy* 1892-1928 (published in 1930), Florence described the events leading up to Emma's death. In July 1912, Hardy had returned from London to Max Gate:

> 'just in time to be at a garden party on July 16 – the last his wife ever gave - which it would have much grieved him afterwards to have missed. The afternoon was sunny and the guests numerous on this final one of many occasions of such a gathering on the lawn there, and nobody foresaw the shadow that was so soon to fall on the house, Mrs Hardy being then, apparently, in her customary health and vigour. In the following month, August, she was at Weymouth for the last time; and Hardy took her and her niece to see the performance of *Bunty* at the Pavilion Theatre. It was her last play.'
>
> 'Bunty Pulls the Strings': A comedy by Scottish actor, director, and playwright Graham Moffat.
>
> 'However, she was noticed to be weaker later on in the autumn, though not ill, and complained of her heart at times. Strangely enough, she one day suddenly sat down to the piano and played a long series of her favourite old tunes, saying at the end she would never play any more. The poem [by Hardy] called *The Last Performance* approximately describes this incident.'[1]

'I am playing my oldest tunes', declared she,
        'All the old tunes I know,—
Those I learnt ever so long ago'.
  – Why she should think just then she'd play them
        Silence cloaks like snow.

When I returned from the town at nightfall
        Notes continued to pour

As when I had left two hours before:
'It's the very last time', she said in closing;
'From now I play no more'.

A few morns onward found her fading,
And, as her life outflew,
I thought of her playing her tunes right through;
And I felt she had known of what was coming,
And wondered how she knew.

In other words, although Emma suspected that she had not long to live, neither Hardy, nor the doctor, suspected as much. Florence continued:

> 'She went out up to the 22nd November, when, though it was a damp, dark afternoon, she motored to pay a visit six miles off. The next day she was distinctly unwell. and the day after that was her birthday, when she seemed depressed. On the 25th two ladies called; and though she consulted with her husband whether or not to go downstairs to see them, and he suggested that she should not in her weak state, she did go down. The strain obliged her to retire immediately they had left. She never went downstairs again.'
>
> 'The next day she agreed to see a doctor, who did not think her seriously ill, but weak from want of nourishment through indigestion.'
>
> 'In the evening she assented quite willingly to Hardy's suggestion that he should go to a rehearsal in Dorchester of a play made by the local company, that he had promised to attend. When he got back at eleven o'clock all the house was in bed and he did not disturb her.'
>
> 'The next morning [27 November 1912] the maid told him in answer to his inquiry that when she had as usual entered Mrs Hardy's room a little earlier she had said she was better, and would probably get up later on; but that she now seemed worse. Hastening to her he was shocked to find her much worse, lying with her eyes closed and unconscious. The doctor came quite quickly, but before he arrived her breathing softened and ceased.'[2] Alice Gale the maid, who was an eyewitness to the entire proceedings, gave a somewhat different account, as will be seen. For everyone excepting Emma, her death, therefore, came almost out of the blue. Said Florence of Emma:

> 'She had not mentioned to her husband, or to anybody else so far as he could discover, that she had any anticipations of death before it occurred so suddenly.'[3]

Hardy had been married to Emma for almost 38 years and the shock to his system was immense. This is reflected in the fact, said Florence, that:

> 'Many poems were written [by him] at the end of the previous year [1912] and the early part of this more than he had ever written before in the same space of time as can be seen by referring to their subjects, as well as to the dates attached to them. To adopt Walpole's words concerning Gray, Hardy was "in flower" in these days, and, like Gray's, his flower was sad-coloured.'[4]

Horace Walpole (1717-1797), writer,
art historian, and politician.
Thomas Gray (1716-1771),
poet and man-of-letters.

Great art often follows great trauma, and this was certainly the case with Hardy, following the present tragic circumstances.

'The funeral was accordingly at Stinsford, a mile from Dorchester and Max Gate, where the Hardys had [been] buried for many years.'[5] Emma was buried in Stinsford churchyard on 30 November 1912; her tomb having been designed by Hardy himself. Hardy's US acquaintance and admirer Rebekah Owen, who attended the funeral, commented on 'the exceeding pathos' of the occasion'.[6]

Chapter 3

Bereavement: The Contribution of Elisabeth Kübler-Ross and David Kessler

In 1969, *On Death and Dying* by Elisabeth Kübler-Ross was published. The book was groundbreaking in that the author described five stages of emotion which the dying patient goes through, namely Denial and Isolation; Anger; Bargaining; Depression; and finally, Acceptance.

In 2005, a follow-up book was published, by Elizabeth Kübler-Ross and David Kessler, entitled *On Grief and Grieving*. Here, the authors made it clear that it was not just the terminally ill patients who went through the five stages of grief. It was also the person who had lost his or her partner and loved one. They pointed out, however, that 'Not everyone goes through all' of these stages in the aforementioned 'prescribed order'.[1] Also, there is often an overlap between the various stages, or in some people, one or more stages are missed out, or it is possible that a person may progress through the various stages, only to regress and enter them again in reverse order.

It was the hope of the authors, they said, that 'this book will become a beacon by shedding light, hope, and comfort on the most difficult time we will all experience in our lives'.[2]

The authors described 'Anticipatory Grief', which occurs when someone we love is expected to die, perhaps of a terminal illness. However, in the case of Hardy, this was not relevant because he had no warning that Emma's life would end so abruptly.

The loss of Emma was by far the most cataclysmic event of Hardy's life. The question was, how did it affect his mindset and how would he manage without her?

Chapter 4

Hardy and the Five Stages of Grief

Stage 1: Denial

'When we are in denial' said Kübler-Ross and Kessler, 'we may respond first by being paralyzed with shock or blanketed with numbness'. But denial is 'not *denial of the actual death*, even though someone may be saying "I can't believe he's dead". The person is actually saying that at first, because it is too much for his or her psyche'.[1]

Deny: to deny is a refusal to acknowledge 'the truth or existence' of a known fact.[2] The term 'denial' therefore implies a wilful refusal to accept the fact of one's partner's death. Therefore, to describe the first stage of grief, a more appropriate term might be 'incomprehension' or 'disbelief'.

> Incomprehension: failure to understand something.[3]
> Disbelief: inability to accept something that is true or real.[4]

The authors gave the example of a lady called Alicia who, when she lost her husband Matthew, 'kept thinking' that his 'death was not real. She couldn't believe it *and* her mind could not fully process it. In this first stage of grieving', said the authors:

> 'We are in a state of shock and denial. We go numb. The denial often comes in the form of a questioning our reality: "Is it true? Did it happen? Are they really gone?" Finally, 'as denial fades, it is slowly replaced with the reality of the loss'.[5]

In his poem *Your Last Drive* (published in December 1912), Hardy recalled Emma's final days. He also alluded to the finality of Emma's death. She had now become a 'ghost', and as such was oblivious to Hardy's thoughts and beyond loving, praising, or censoring him.

Ghost: an apparition of a dead person which is believed to appear or become manifest to the living, typically as a nebulous image.[6]

Here by the moorway you returned,
And saw the borough lights ahead
That lit your face — all undiscerned
To be in a week the face of the dead,
And you told of the charm of that haloed view
That never again would beam on you.

And on your left you passed the spot
Where eight days later you were to lie,
And be spoken of as one who was not;
Beholding it with a cursory eye
As alien from you, though under its tree
You soon would halt everlastingly.

I drove not with you…. Yet had I sat
At your side that eve I should not have seen
That the countenance I was glancing at
Had a last-time look in the flickering sheen,
Nor have read the writing upon your face,
'I go hence soon to my resting-place;

'You may miss me then. But I shall not know
How many times you visit me there,
Or what your thoughts are, or if you go
There never at all. And I shall not care.
Should you censure me I shall take no heed
And even your praises I shall not need.'

True: never you'll know. And you will not mind.
But shall I then slight you because of such?
Dear ghost, in the past did you ever find
Me one whom consequence influenced much?
Yet the fact indeed remains the same,
You are past love, praise, indifference, blame.

Moorway: the road across the moor.

'The spot' referred to is Stinsford Churchyard.

To poet, author, and critic Edmund Gosse on 17 December 1912, Hardy wrote of Emma's death as follows:

> 'It was so good of you & Mrs Gosse to write. What do you say on the incredibility of this event I feel even now - it seeming sometimes for a moment that it cannot have happened, & that I shall see her coming in from the garden with a little trowel in her hand, after pottering among the plants as she used to do.'[7]

To Lady Ilchester, Anglo-Irish noblewoman and leading figure in London society on 21 January 1913, Hardy wrote of Emma's death:

> 'It was so unexpected that even now I sometimes think for a moment that it cannot have happened, & that she may come in from the garden saying that the snowdrops & crocuses are peeping up.'[8]

In other words, Hardy was still in a state of disbelief.

Stage 2: Anger

'This stage presents itself in many ways', said Kübler-Ross and Kessler, for example:

> 'anger at your loved one that he [or she] didn't take better care of himself or anger that you didn't take better care of him.[9] Maybe you are angry that God didn't take better care of your loved one.[10] [And] Underneath anger is pain, *your* pain. It is natural to feel deserted and abandoned.'[11]

In his poem *A Death-Day Recalled* (published in 1914), Hardy appears to have expressed his anger that nature is indifferent to Emma's passing and that, instead, life goes on as usual.

> Beeny did not quiver,
> Juliot grew not gray,
> Thin Valency's river
> Held its wonted way.
> Bos seemed not to utter
> Dimmest note of dirge,
> Targan mouth a mutter
> To its creamy surge.

Yet though these, unheeding,
Listless, passed the hour
Of her spirit's speeding,
She had, in her flower,
Sought and loved the places -
Much and often pined
For their lonely faces
When in towns confined.

Why did not Valency
In his purl deplore
One whose haunts were whence he
Drew his limpid store?
Why did Bos not thunder
Targan apprehend
Body and breath were sunder
Of their former friend?

Beeny Cliff: 1 mile north-west of St Julitta's Rectory; Juliot: St Julitta's Church, situated on the northern slopes of the Valency Valley, 2 miles east of Boscastle Harbour, where the river Valency reaches the sea; Valency: the River; Bos: Boscastle and its headlands; Targan: Pentargan Bay, 1 mile east of St Julitta's Rectory.

Stage 3: Bargaining

'Before a loss', said Kübler-Ross and Kessler:

> 'it seems you will do anything if only your loved one may be spared. "Please, God", you bargain, "I will never be angry at my wife again if you'll just let her live".'[12]

Bargain: an agreement between two of more people (in this case Hardy and God) … as to what each with do for the other.

This, however, is irrelevant as far as Hardy was concerned, as he had no notion that his wife was going to die so suddenly.

'Guilt is often bargaining's companion', said the authors:

> 'The "if onlys" cause us to find fault with ourselves and what we "think" we could have done differently. We may even bargain

> with the pain. We will do anything not to feel the pain of this loss. We remain in the past, trying to negotiate our way out of the hurt.'[13]

In his poem *Rain on a Grave* (composed on New Year's Eve, 31 January 1913, and published in 1914), Hardy expressed the wish that it was he who had died, and not Emma, or that they both had died together. This was a bargain that he would gladly have made, whereby he would have avoided the heartache of losing Emma:

> III
> Would that I lay there
>   And she were housed here!
> Or better, together
> Were folded away there
> Exposed to one weather
> We both, — who would stray there
> When sunny the day there,
>   Or evening was clear
>   At the prime of the year.
>
> IV
> Soon will be growing
>   Green blades from her mound,
> And daisies be showing
>   Like stars on the ground,
> Till she form part of them —
> Ay — the sweet heart of them,
> Loved beyond measure
> With a child's pleasure
>   All her life's round.

Hardy's use of imagery – daisies like stars' – to make a poignant point is delightful and unsurpassed!

Stage 4: Depression

In the Fourth Stage of Loss, said Kübler-Ross and Kessler:

> 'Empty feelings present themselves, and grief enters our lives on a deeper level, deeper than we ever imagined. This depressive

> stage feels as though it will last forever. We withdraw from life, left in a fog of intense sadness, wondering perhaps, if there is any point in going on alone. Why go on at all? Life seems pointless.'[14]

In his poem *End of The Year 1912* (composed immediately after the death of Emma on 27 November of that year, and published in 1922), Hardy described himself as a broken man, whose life was now ruined.

> You were here at his young beginning,
> You are not here at his aged end;
> Off he coaxed you from Life's mad spinning,
> Lest you should see his form extend
> Shivering, sighing,
> Slowly dying,
> And a tear on him expend.
>
> So it comes that we stand lonely
> In the star-lit avenue,
> Dropping broken lipwords only,
> For we hear no songs from you,
> Such as flew here
> For the new year
> Once, while six bells swung thereto.

Hardy always 'sat up' to enjoy the sound of Dorchester's church bells, as they rang in each new year.

To poet and novelist Florence Henniker on 17 December 1912, the month after Emma's death, Hardy wrote:

> 'In spite of the differences between us … my life is intensely sad to me now without her. The saddest moments of all are when I go into the garden & to that long straight walk at the top that you know where she used to walk every evening just before dusk, the cat trotting faithfully behind her; & at times when I almost expect to see her as usual coming in from the flower-beds with a little trowel in her hand.'[15]

Anyone who has lost a beloved partner will immediately understand such sentiments of Hardy's, where memories come flooding back, clutching at one like the tentacles of an octopus and dragging one down into the black, sunless pit of despair.

Hardy's poem *It Never Looks like Summer* was composed on 8 March 1913, which was the fourth month after Emma's death. It was published in 1917 and in that year, accompanied by his second wife Florence, he revisited Boscastle. In the poem, Hardy revealed the depth of his sadness and depression, in comparison with the times when he had first visited Emma in Cornwall, when it had always seemed like summer.

> 'It never looks like summer here
> On Beeny by the sea.'
> But though she saw its look as drear,
> Summer it seemed to me.
>
> It never looks like summer now
> Whatever weather's there;
> But ah, it cannot anyhow,
> On Beeny or elsewhere!

In his poem *The Difference* (published in 1914) Hardy mourned for his former 'heartmate' Emma and alluded to the transient nature of love:

> Sinking down by the gate I discern the thin moon,
> And a blackbird tries over old airs in the pine,
> But the moon is a sorry one, sad the bird's tune,
> For this spot is unknown to that Heartmate of mine.
>
> Did my Heartmate but haunt here at times such as now,
> The song would be joyous and cheerful the moon;
> But she will see never this gate, path, or bough,
> Nor I find a joy in the scene or the tune.

Although Hardy made great efforts to revisit the places that he and Emma had visited together, he clearly had begun to find the remembrance which such visits evoked to be increasingly painful to him.

Stage 5: Acceptance

Acceptance, the final stage of grieving, said Kübler-Ross and Kessler:

> 'is often confused with the notion of being all right or okay with what happened. This is not the case. Most people don't ever feel okay or all right about the loss of a loved one. This stage is about

> accepting the reality that our loved one is physically going and recognizing this new reality is the permanent reality. We will never like this reality or make it okay, but eventually we accept it. We learn to live with it. It is the new norm with which we must learn to live. This is where our final healing and adjustment can take a firm hold, despite the fact that healing often looks and feels like an unattainable state.'[16]

In this, the authors showed great insight in acknowledging that for some, despite reaching the point of acceptance the pain of loss never abates.

In his poem *Old Excursions* (composed in April 1913 and published in 1917), Hardy accepted that Emma was lost to him forever. Nonetheless, he asked himself if it did him good to revisit the former haunts that he and Emma used to frequent, and he decided that, despite the aforementioned pain of remembrance, by and large it did. This was because, at these locations, he felt close to his deceased wife, who he imagined to be scolding him for being miserable about it!

> 'What's the good of going to Ridgeway,
> Cerne, or Sydling Mill,
> Or to Yell'ham Hill,
> Blithely bearing Casterbridge-way
> As we used to do?
> She will no more climb up there,
> Or be visible anywhere
> In those haunts we knew.'
>
> But to-night, while walking weary,
> Near me seemed her shade,
> Come as 'twere to upbraid
> This my mood in deeming dreary
> Scenes that used to please;
> And, if she did come to me,
> Still solicitous, there may be
> Good in going to these.
>
> So, I'll care to roam to Ridgeway,
> Cerne, or Sydling Mill,
> Or to Yell'ham Hill,
> Blithely bearing Casterbridge-way
> As we used to do,
> Since her phasm may flit out there,

And may greet me anywhere
In those haunts we knew.

'Casterbridge': Hardy's name for Dorchester.

Shade: shadow.[17]

On 21 August 1913, the 11th month after Emma's death, Florence reported to banker, writer, and anthropologist Edward Clodd that Hardy was 'in good health, & wonderfully cheerful. He has had no fit of depression for quite a long time'.[18] This implies that Hardy had accepted the loss of Emma. And yet, on 3 December 1915 Florence told Rebekah Owen that, to her 'great dismay', Hardy had reverted to his former self. 'Tom … says he feels that he never wants to go anywhere or see anyone again. He wants to live on here [at Max Gate], quite quietly, shut up in his study.'[19]

Kübler-Ross and Kessler were adamant that a person eventually accepts the fact of the loss of their partner. However, for Hardy, and doubtless for millions of others, this does not appear to be the case. After all, unless one possesses a religious faith, *how can one* accept the loss of a beloved soulmate, lover, companion, etc, and the fact that life has suddenly become a hideous, lonely, soul-destroying void? Did Hardy *ever* achieve peace of mind after his bereavement, and if so, how? This will be discussed shortly.

Chapter 5

Hardy and the Inner World of Grief

In their book *On Grief and Grieving*, Kübler-Ross and Kessler proceeded to enumerate specific aspects of grief, which they included under three headings: 'The Inner World of Grief'; 'The Outer World of Grief', and 'Specific Circumstances'. Under the heading 'The Inner World of Grief', the authors included several subheadings, including the following:

1. Your Loss

Said Kübler-Ross and Kessler:

> 'An unimaginable, indescribable loss has taken place. It has inflicted a wound so deep that numbness and excruciating pain are the material of which it is made.'
>
> 'Everyone experiences many losses throughout life, but the death of a loved one is unmatched for its emptiness and profound sadness. Your world stops.' However, 'Your life continues, but you are not sure why. A different life appears before you, one in which your loved one will no longer be physically present. No one can give you words to make you feel better. There are none. You will survive, though you may not be sure how or even if you want to.'

In fact, for some the loss is so overwhelming that they do not survive, either through self-neglect or by taking their own lives.

> 'Your loss and the grief that accompanies it are very personal, different from anyone else's. Others may share the experience of their losses. They may try to console you in the only way they know. But your loss stands alone in its meaning to you, in its painful uniqueness.'
>
> 'You are the only one who can survey the magnitude of your loss. No one will ever know the meaning of what was shared, the

deepest of the void that shadows your future. You alone know your loss. Only you can fully appreciate the depth of the physical relationship that has ended. You knew your loved one in a way that no one else ever did or ever will.'[1]

Hardy was a great one for remembering anniversaries, the anniversary of Emma's death being, for him, the saddest of them all.

In his poem *The Lament of the Looking-Glass* (published in 1922), Hardy bewailed the fact that he would never again behold such beauty as Emma possessed:

Words from the mirror softly pass
To the curtains with a sigh:
'Why should I trouble again to glass
These smileless things hard by,
Since she I pleasured once, alas,
Is now no longer nigh!'

'I've imaged shadows of coursing cloud,
And of the plying limb
On the pensive pine when the air is loud
With its aerial hymn;
But never do they make me proud
To catch them within my rim!

'I flash back phantoms of the night
That sometimes flit by me,
I echo roses red and white -
The loveliest blooms that be -
But now I never hold to sight
So sweet a flower as she.'

Rim: upper or outer edge of an object.[2]

To pleasure: to give sexual enjoyment or satisfaction to.[3]

'Satisfaction' is probably the operative word here, rather than 'sexual enjoyment', since as already mentioned, it is likely that Hardy's marriage was never consummated.

Ghost: an apparition of a dead person which is believed to appear or become manifest to the living, typically as a nebulous image.[4]

Thomas Hardy and the Death of Emma

In his poem *Days to Recollect* (published in 1925), Hardy recalled a wonderful visit that he and Emma had made to St Alban's (Aldhelm's) Head in Dorset's Isle of Purbeck, and he revealed his unutterable sadness at her subsequent death. If only she was still alive, so they could have continued to share the memory!

Do you recall
That day in Fall
When we walked towards Saint Alban's Head,
On thistledown that summer had shed,
Or must I remind you?
Winged thistle-seeds which hitherto
Had lain as none were there, or few,
But rose at the brush of your petticoat-seam
(As ghosts might rise of the recent dead),
And sailed on the breeze in a nebulous stream
Like a comet's tail behind you:
You don't recall
That day in Fall?

Then do you remember
That sad November
When you left me never to see me more,
And looked quite other than theretofore,
As if it could not be you?
And lay by the window whence you had gazed
So many times when blamed or praised,
Morning or noon, through years and years,
Accepting the gifts that Fortune bore,
Sharing, enduring, joys, hopes, fears!
Well: I never more did see you. —
Say you remember
That sad November!

In his poem *I Found Her out There* (published in 1914), Hardy reminisced about first meeting Emma, and now that she had passed away, about the joys that she had once enjoyed but could now no longer experience, including listening to the sound of the sea.

I found her out there
On a slope few see,
That falls westwardly
To the salt-edged air,

Where the ocean breaks
On the purple strand,
And the hurricane shakes
The solid land.

I brought her here,
And have laid her to rest
In a noiseless nest
No sea beats near.
She will never be stirred
In her loamy cell
By the waves long heard
And loved so well.

So she does not sleep
By those haunted heights
The Atlantic smites
And the blind gales sweep,
Whence she often would gaze
At Dundagel's famed head,
While the dipping blaze
Dyed her face fire-red;

And would sigh at the tale
Of sunk Lyonesse,
As a wind-tugged tress
Flapped her cheek like a flail
Or listen at whiles
With a thought-bound brow
To the murmuring miles
She is far from now.

Yet her shade, maybe,
Will creep underground
Till it catch the sound
Of that western sea
As it swells and sobs
Where she once domiciled,
And joy in its throbs
With the heart of a child.

Dundagel: Hardy's name for Tintagel.

In other words, Hardy was thinking unselfishly, not only of his own loss, but also of Emma, and the pleasures that she had once enjoyed, but was now no longer able to partake of.

2. Relief

Said Kübler-Ross and Kessler:

> 'For many, a strange and unexpected feeling sits amid the loss: a feeling of relief that contrasts with the pervading sadness. It feels out of place, out of step, and is often considered wrong. Why would you feel a sense of relief at the loss of someone so close and so dear?'
>
> 'If you feel relief, it may be because your loved one was suffering, and you are grateful it has ended. Watching or even thinking about a loved one's suffering places a heavy pain on top of the sadness.'[6]

Emma, by all accounts, was unwell for a long period prior to her untimely death, but she kept her suffering to herself so Hardy was hardly aware of it. Did Hardy feel relief that Emma's suffering had come to an end? In fact, her final illness had been so brief that Hardy had not appreciated the seriousness of it. Therefore, it was probably only at the very end when he became fully aware of the true extent and gravity of Emma's pain and distress.

3. Emotional Rest

Said Kübler-Ross and Kessler:

> 'People experience a wide range of emotions after a loss, from not caring, to being on edge, to feeling angry or sad about everything. We can go from feeling okay to feeling devastated in a minute without warning. We can have mood swings that are hard for anyone around us to comprehend, because even we don't understand them. One minute we are okay. The next we're in tears. This is how grief works.'[7]

According to Florence, Hardy did indeed exhibit a degree of emotional lability after the death of Emma, reflecting an inner turmoil which never completely abated.

There is another dimension to this, a physiological one. This will be discussed shortly.

4. Regrets

Said Kübler-Ross and Kessler:

> 'When a loved one dies, we are often left with many regrets about all those things we wish we had said, all those things we wish we had done. We may regret what we didn't do or didn't say. We keep going back over things we wish we'd said and things we wish we hadn't. We are all human. There are very few people who can say they don't have even a small regret. Regrets are part of loss, and you are not alone in the experience of regret.'[8]

On 12 December 1912, Hardy wrote to Ellen, wife of his friend Edmund Gosse, to say of the recently departed Emma:

> 'Probably nobody in London knew her better than you did, & when I think of the innumerable times we have shared your hospitality it is sad in the extreme to feel that we shall never do so again together.'
>
> 'I have been full of regrets that I did not at all foresee the possibility of her passing away thus, but merely thought her few days of illness a temporary ailment which I need not be anxious about. Everybody, myself included, supposed her to have a high vitality & the soundest of constitutions.'[9]

To Florence Henniker on 17 July 1914, Hardy wrote:

> 'As you are kind enough to write about that little poem called *Before and After Summer*, I remember to tell you that I am collecting the pieces in verse that I have written since the last volume of poetry was published & looking them over with a view of bringing them out some when towards the end of the year. Some of them I rather shrink from printing – those I wrote just after Emma died, when I looked back at her as she had originally been, & when I felt miserable lest I had not treated considerately in her latter life. However, I shall publish as the only amends I can make.'[10]

In his poem *Ten Years Since* (composed in November 1922, ten years to the month after Emma had died, and published in 1925), Hardy appeared to be saying that he wished that he had paid more attention to Emma in the weeks and months before she died.

'Tis ten years since
I saw her on the stairs,
Heard her in house-affairs,
And listened to her cares;
And the trees are ten feet taller,
And the sunny spaces smaller
Whose bloomage would enthrall her;
And the piano wires are rustier,
The smell of bindings mustier,
And lofts and lumber dustier
Than when, with casual look
And ear, light note I took
Of what shut like a book
Those ten years since!

Bloomage: the blossoms or bloom of a plant or area taken collectively.

5. Tears

Said Kübler-Ross and Kessler:

> 'Tears are one of the many ways we release our sadness, one of our many wondrous built-in healing mechanisms. Unfortunately, too often we try to stop this necessary and primal release of our emotions. In grief we often have only two main thoughts about crying. The first is the overwhelming force of sadness that hits us. The second is "I must stop crying".'[11]

On 19 July 1917 Hardy wrote to author and editor George A. B. Dewar to say:

> 'I am so pleased to hear that you will not soon forget the Beeny Cliff poems. They were written at a time of deep sadness.'[12]

Did Hardy ever shed tears? Given his sensitive nature, it seems extremely likely that he did, though no one evidently recorded such an event.

6. Angels

Said Kübler-Ross and Kessler:

> 'Some people have strong beliefs in angels, guardian angels, while others hope they exist.'

Guardian angel: a spirit that is thought to watch over and protect a person or place.[13]

> 'We speak of them in many forms in our culture: the angel of death, angels we pray to for help and comfort.'

Angel of Death: a spiritual soul responsible to comfort people when they are dying and safely carry their souls into an afterlife.[14]

Spiritual: relating to or affecting the human spirit or soul as opposed to material or physical things.[15]

Soul: the spiritual or immaterial part of a human being or animal, regarded as immortal.[16]

Afterlife: life after death.[17]

'Sometimes they are just a part of our God and the heavens. We ask them to be gentle as they take our loved one. We ask them to watch over us. We ask them to meet our loved ones on the other side [i.e. in the next life]. Many times, we just ask for their help. It is unnecessary to debate the reality of angels. They are beyond an entity that can be proved or disproved. Many believe you cannot die alone, that angels are always present.'[18]

Although Hardy was an atheist, in the traditional sense of the word, he made reference to an angel in his poem *The Face at the Casement* (published in 1914):

> And that the suffer said,
> For her call no words could thank her;
> As his angel he must rank her
> Till life's spark fled.

Atheism: the theory or belief that God does not exist.[19]

God: in Christianity and other monotheistic religions, the creator and ruler of the universe and source of all moral authority; the supreme being. In certain other religions, a superhuman being or spirit worshipped as having power over nature or human fortunes.[20]

Hardy regarded 'God', or in his words, 'The Will', as being amoral as far as humans were concerned, and therefore certainly not an entity who was worthy of worship!

Likewise in his poem *The Lacking Sense* (published in 1901), Hardy referred to an 'angel fallen from grace'.

7. Dreams

Said Kübler-Ross and Kessler:

> 'Dreams are a natural part of sleep. They embody our hopes, our worst fears, and everything in between. After a loss, it is not unusual to dream that your loved one is still alive.'[21] However, 'Even if dreams of loss truthfully reflect the circumstances around loss, they rarely follow the actual events. A long struggle may produce a dream about finding your way through the darkness in the forest to get to your loved one.'[22]

In his poem *The Dream is – Which?* (composed in March 1913, which was the fourth month after Emma's death, and published in 1922), Hardy described rural pursuits and dancing, such as he had enjoyed with Emma in those early days, as now being akin to a dream, and he agonized over the fact that they would enjoy them together no more:

> I am laughing by the brook with her,
> Splashed in its tumbling stir;
> And then it is a blankness looms
> As if I walked not there,
> Nor she, but found me in haggard rooms,
> And treading a lonely stair.
>
> With radiant cheeks and rapid eyes
> We sit where none espies;
> Till a harsh change comes edging in
> As no such scene were there,
> But winter, and I were bent and thin,
> And cinder-gray my hair.
>
> We dance in heys around the hall,
> Weightless as thistleball;
> And then a curtain drops between,

As if I danced not there,
But wandered through a mounded green
To find her, I knew where.

Heys: reels.[23]

Thistleball: a thistle in the shape of a ball.[24]

Mounded: a burial mound marking her grave.

Likewise, in his poem *A Dream or No* (published in 1914), Hardy, who was perpetually agonizing over the death of Emma, asked himself, was the time when he first set eyes on her at St Juliot in Cornwall merely a dream, and was the entire local landscape merely a dream?

Why go to Saint-Juliot? What's Juliot to me?
I've been but made fancy
By some necromancy
That much of my life claims the spot as its key.

Yes. I have had dreams of that place in the West,
And a maiden abiding
Thereat as in hiding;
Fair-eyed and white-shouldered, broad-browed and brown-tressed.

And of how, coastward bound on a night long ago,
There lonely I found her,
The sea-birds around her,
And other than nigh things uncaring to know.

So sweet her life there (in my thought has it seemed)
That quickly she drew me
To take her unto me,
And lodge her long years with me. Such have I dreamed.

But nought of that maid from Saint-Juliot I see;
Can she ever have been here,
And shed her life's sheen here,
The woman I thought a long housemate with me?

Does there even a place like Saint-Juliot exist?
Or a Vallency Valley
With stream and leafed alley,
Or Beeny, or Bos with its flounce flinging mist?

Necromancy: the supposed practice of communicating with the dead, especially in order to predict the future.[25]

8. Roles

Said Kübler-Ross and Kessler:

> 'When a loved one dies, all the roles they fulfilled all left open [i.e. unfulfilled].'[26]

What part, if any, Emma played in the running of the household at Max Gate in her later years is not known, but as she lived in rooms in the attic, it is likely that these duties largely devolved to the housemaid and cook. As for Hardy, his principal role in life was, of course, that of a writer. However, from the accounts of the household staff, he was a demanding employer – something of an unsmiling martinet, in fact - who insisted on smartness and efficiency. When Florence appeared on the scene, it is likely that she too became involved in the running of the Hardy household, so Hardy's life, from a practical point of view, would have remained largely undisturbed.

9. The Story

Said Kübler-Ross and Kessler:

> 'Now you sit alone remembering the story of your loss. You may find yourself retelling the story to friends and family. Immediately following the loss, everyone wants to know how it happened. You tell your tale through sadness and tears. When friends come to visit you discuss the parts of the story you continue to grapple with. As time passes, however, you may see others grow weary of hearing the story, although you are not yet tired of telling it.'
> However, for the bereaved person:
> 'Telling the story is part of the healing of a traumatic event. [This] helps to dissipate the pain. Telling your story often and in detail is primal to the grieving process. You must get it out. Grief must be witnessed to be healed. Grief shared is grief abated.'

For Hardy, of course, telling his story meant telling it to the whole world, though in his poetry he did not always make it obvious that he and Emma were the protagonists of the poems. And the very act of writing poems in memory of Emma may well have been a catharsis for him – a coping mechanism which helped him to deal with the pain.

Also, said Kübler-Ross and Kessler:

> 'Support and bereavement groups are important, not only because they allow you to be with others who have experienced loss, but because they provide another forum for talking about the devastating events that befell your world. Tell your tale, because it reinforces that your loss mattered.'[27]

Alas, no such support groups existed in Hardy's time. Instead, he was supported by Florence, who was devoted to him, and also by his three siblings, Mary, Henry, and Kate.

10. Fault

In respect of the person who has been bereaved, said Kübler-Ross and Kessler: 'It feels as if it was somehow your fault.' However, unless the death of your loved one was the result of:

> 'a violent crime or gross neglect, no one is to blame. We are responsible for our health, but we are not the ones to blame for our illnesses.'[28]

Hardy, however, *did* feel that he was at fault in regard to the death of Emma, by his neglect of her, as will be seen. Continued Kübler-Ross and Kessler:

> 'People are often conflicted about the loss of loved ones. We mourn for those who cared for us the way they should have. We also mourn for those who did not give us the love we deserved. You can grieve fully for people who were terrible to you. And if you need to grieve for them, you should do so. We must take time to mourn and experience our losses and acknowledge the reality that those losses cannot be negated, even if we think the person did not deserve our love.'[29]

Hardy was at pains not to blame Emma for her recurrent mental 'aberrations', in public at any rate, but was this the whole story? Did he inwardly feel resentful?

11. Resentment

Resentment is defined as bitter indignation at having been treated unfairly.[30] Did Hardy resent the fact that Emma, in her later years, failed to provide him with the love, kindness, and companionship that he so desired? Even though he was at pains to state that Emma's mental 'aberration' was in no way her fault, in private he undoubtedly resented the fact that as a wife, she had ultimately failed in all respects, to come up to his expectations. This smouldering resentment, which is evident in his poems, would have compounded his sense of loss and made his grief more acute and more poignant. The phrase 'between them lay a sword' in particular comes to mind, from his aforementioned poem *To a Sea-Cliff*.

Continued Kübler-Ross and Kessler:

> 'Resentment doesn't always die with death. It can be a common part of unfinished business we are left with. Resentment is old anger that we never dealt with or had the chance to deal with.'[31] Nevertheless, you can still:
>
> 'grieve fully for people who were terrible to you. And if you need to grieve for them, you should do so.' Finally, the authors concluded:
>
> 'We must take time to mourn and experience our losses and acknowledge the reality that those losses cannot be negated even if we think the person did not deserve our love.'[32]

And yet Hardy's poems indicate that he was *never again at peace*, after the death of Emma.

12. Other Losses

Said Kübler-Ross and Kessler:

> 'You may have lost your beloved, but the grief brings into your awareness all the losses that have occurred in your life, past and present.'[33]

Surely, the loss of Emma put Hardy in mind of his late parents, together with that of other late relatives and friends, whom he would have mourned also. This is reflected in his poem *Paying Calls* (published in 1917):

> I went by footpath and by stile
> Beyond where bustle ends,
> Strayed here a mile and there a mile
> And called upon some friends.

On certain ones I had not seen
For years past did I call,
And then on others who had been
The oldest friends of all.

It was the time of midsummer
When they had used to roam;
But now, though tempting was the air,
I found them all at home.

I spoke to one and other of them
By path and stone and tree
Of things we had done ere days were dim,
But they spoke not to me.

13. Life Beliefs

After the death of a loved one, said Kübler-Ross and Kessler:

> 'Your belief system needs to heal and regroup as much as your soul does. You must start to rebuild a new belief system from the foundation up, one that has room for the realities of life and still offers safety and hope for a different life: a belief system that will ultimately have a beauty of its own to be discovered with life and loss.'[34]

Clearly, Kübler-Ross and Kessler had a belief system. Many others, however, have no such belief systems.

Dogma: a principle or set of principles laid down by an authority as incontrovertibly true.[35]

In his poem *The Impercipient* - one who fails to perceive something[36] (composed after he had attended a service in a cathedral, and published in 1898), Hardy confessed that he did not embrace the faith and belief of the other worshippers, and derived no comfort from the Christian faith:

I
That from this bright believing band
    An outcast I should be,
That faiths by which my comrades stand
    Seem fantasies to me,

And mirage-mists their Shining Land,
    Is a drear destiny.

II

Why thus my soul should be consigned
    To infelicity,
Why always I must feel as blind
    To sights my brethren see,
Why joys they've found I cannot find,
    Abides a mystery.

III

Since heart of mine knows not that ease
    Which they know; since it be
That He who breathes All's Well to these
    Breathes no All's Well to me,
My lack might move their sympathies
    And Christian charity!

In his poem *On a Fine Morning* (published in 1901), Hardy described how he clung on to hope, and tried to be optimistic, and believe that Earth was created for man by a benign creator:

Whence comes Solace? - Not from seeing
What is doing, suffering, being,
Not from noting Life's conditions,
Nor from heeding Time's monitions;
    But in cleaving to the Dream,
    And in gazing at the gleam
    Whereby gray things golden seem.

Thus do I this heyday, holding
Shadows but as lights unfolding,
As no specious show this moment
With its irised embowment;
    But as nothing other than
    Part of a benignant plan;
    Proof that earth was made for man.

Benignant: kindly and benevolent.[37]
Embowment: an arch or vault.

In his poem *New Year's Eve* (composed in 1906, and published in 1909), Hardy questioned why God had created the Earth, and why He had created sentient human beings. After all, if we had not been born then the question of whether we desired to have joy in our lives would not have arisen. And in reply, God admitted that he had been very short-sighted!

I
'I have finished another year,' said God,
'In grey, green, white, and brown;
I have strewn the leaf upon the sod,
Sealed up the worm within the clod,
And let the last sun down.'

II
'And what's the good of it?' I said.
'What reasons made you call
From formless void this earth we tread,
When nine-and-ninety can be read
Why nought should be at all?

III
'Yea, Sire; why shaped you us, "who in
This tabernacle groan" – [38]
If ever a joy be found herein,
Such joy no man had wished to win
If he had never known!'

Hardy biographer Evelyn Hardy summed up the situation perfectly in respect of Hardy and 'God'. Said she, 'Many of his notes and poems' were:

> 'concerned with this theme — that of a repentant Creator who should be brought to task for the suffering he has permitted, if not actually caused, who sees his error and mends his ways.'[39]

Hardy was not the first to question 'God', nor was he the last. In the *Old Testament's* Book of Psalms, for instance, there are several examples, as Hardy himself may have been well aware:

> 'Why, Lord, do you stand far off?
> Why do you hide yourself in times of trouble?'
> Psalm 10, verse 1.

'I say to God my Rock,
"Why have you forgotten me?
Why must I go about mourning,
oppressed by the enemy?"

My bones suffer mortal agony
as my foes taunt me,
saying to me all day long,
"Where is your God?"'

Psalm 42, verse 9,10.

'Awake, Lord! Why do you sleep?
Rouse yourself! Do not reject us forever.
Why do you hide your face
and forget our misery and oppression?'

Psalm 44, verse 24.

In his poem *Fragment* (published in 1917), Hardy pondered over the nature of 'God'. He revealed that to some, himself included, 'God' was synonymous with 'The Will'; 'A Force'; 'The Law'; or 'The Ultimate Cause'. And he imagined those who were between life and death asking God please to bring them up to date with current happenings on Earth:

I
At last I entered a long dark gallery,
Catacomb-lined; and ranged at the side
Were the bodies of men from far and wide
Who, motion past, were nevertheless not dead.

II
'The sense of waiting here strikes strong;
Everyone's waiting, waiting, it seems to me;
What are you waiting for so long? —
What is to happen?' I said.

III
'O we are waiting for one called God,' said they,
'(Though by some the Will, or Force, or Laws;
And, vaguely, by some, the Ultimate Cause;)
Waiting for him to see us before we are clay.
Yes; waiting, waiting, for God to know it.' …

IV
'To know what?' questioned I.
'To know how things have been going on earth and below it ...

In the 'Afterscene: The Overworld', of Hardy's closet drama (one intended to be read rather than performed) *The Dynasts* (published in three parts, in 1904, 1906, and 1908), the 'Spirit Ironic' refers to:

... a dreaming, dark, dumb Thing
That turns the handle of this idle show

In other words, Hardy was extremely scornful of whoever or whatever 'higher being' it was that, or so he believed, presided over events that took place upon the earth.

In one of his most famous poems entitled *The Oxen* (composed in 1915, and published in 1917), Hardy expressed his doubts about Christianity and the Christian message, and yet, despite all, he could not help wishing and hoping that it might be true. And of course, if it was true, then Hardy could look forward to being reunited with Emma in the afterlife, provided of course that they both had been admitted to heaven!

Christmas Eve, and twelve of the clock.
"Now they are all on their knees,"
An elder said as we sat in a flock
By the embers in hearthside ease.

We pictured the meek mild creatures where
They dwelt in their strawy pen,
Nor did it occur to one of us there
To doubt they were kneeling then.

So fair a fancy few would weave
In these years! Yet, I feel,
If someone said on Christmas Eve,
"Come; see the oxen kneel,

"In the lonely barton by yonder coomb
Our childhood used to know,"
I should go with him in the gloom,
Hoping it might be so.

Barton: farmyard.

In other words, if the Christian message *was* true, then those who had lived good and blameless lives could hope for immortality and reunification with their loved ones. So perhaps Hardy did wonder - hope even – that when he himself died, he and Emma would be reunited.

In his poem *Intra Sepulchrum* - 'Within the Tomb' (published in 1922), Hardy alluded to the fact that whereas Emma was a Christian and a believer, he was not, even though he pretended to her that he was! But of course, from the sentiments expressed by Hardy in his novels and poems, Emma would have known full well that he was an atheist.

I
What curious things we said,
What curious things we did
Up there in the world we walked till dead
Our kith and kin amid!

II
How we played at love,
And its wildness, weakness, woe;
Yes, played thereat far more than enough
As it turned out, I trow!

III
Played at believing in gods
And observing the ordinances,
I for your sake in impossible codes
Right ready to acquiesce.

Trow: think or believe.[40]

14. Isolation

Said Kübler-Ross and Kessler:

> 'You are alone. There is a war now where none existed before, standing between you and the rest of the world. But your isolation is not related to your surroundings or the people in your world. You can be in a large group of friends and relatives feel as disconnected as if you were lost in the desert. There is no port in the storm, and the one person who could bring you connection is the person who is gone forever. And so, you feel you will be forever lost.'

> 'You have entered an abnormal, lonely, and unwelcome new world where are you are nothing but an island of sadness. And so far, there is no way out, no matter what anybody else wants for you.'[41]
>
> 'Isolation feels like being in a room with no doors or windows - a place with no way out. And the longer you get stuck there, the harder it becomes to share the pain and sorrow that create the portals for your movement into the next phase of grief. In isolation, hope disappears, despair rules, and you can no longer glimpse a life beyond the invisible walls that imprison you.'[42]

Hardy must surely have felt such isolation, as he rattled around in his large mansion, Max Gate, alone apart from the servants, pets, and the occasional visit from Florence. And yet somehow, despite his overwhelming grief, he survived. But how? This question will be addressed shortly.

15. Secrets

Said Kübler-Ross and Kessler:

> 'After a loved one had died it is not unusual to uncover a secret or two here or there. The hardest part is that the secret represents something we perceive as them [the departed loved one] withholding from us personally. A tremendous shock arises when a secret is discovered.'[43] Emma withheld such a secret from Hardy, and when he discovered that, during their marriage, she had been writing secret criticisms of him, he would surely have been shocked to the core.

For a bereaved person, what he or she dreads is the discovery of some message from his or her late beloved which contains elements of criticism or reproach. For there is now no opportunity to make amends or for reconciliation. Sure enough, said Flower, 'Some days after' Emma's funeral, Hardy:

> 'went to her room and discovered there two big manuscripts she had written. Book-length manuscripts. One was entitled: *The Pleasures of Heaven and the Pains of Hell*. The second bore the title: *What I Think of My Husband*. He began to read them. The core of their tragedy lay in these written sheets.'
>
> 'Presently he ceased to read. He lit the fire in the grate. When the flames blazed up he tore the manuscripts into their pages and dropped them into the fire one by one ....'[44] By contrast, Hardy:

> 'also found those fresh and charming *Recollections* [a book by Emma which will be discussed shortly], written the year before she died [in which her] mind had gone back to those Cornish days; in her own simple manner she had recaptured their magic, a discovery which must have brought him comfort.'[45]

So, Emma *had once been happy* in Hardy's company, as he had once been blissfully happy in hers.

The discovery by Hardy of letters and notebooks of Emma's that were critical of him must have shocked and dismayed him. To lose Emma was one thing; to be upbraided by her posthumously would have been an added and sickening body blow.

16. Punishment

Said Kübler-Ross and Kessler:

> 'What did you do so wrong to deserve this kind of punishment? What did your loved one ever do to deserve their illness and death? Nothing. But that does not stop us from feeling punished. For some, the idea of punishment may come from religion and a God that punishes. Actions have consequences, but as counselors we do not believe that loss comes from punishment.'[46]

Hardy, however, believed that the death of Emma *was* a punishment upon him. In his poem *The Torn Letter* (published in 1914), the narrator was, of course, Hardy, and the unknown woman was, of course, Emma. Emma complained of Hardy's derision of her, whereas he admitted that he was 'out of order', and blamed himself for the fact that what he termed 'The Will' had decided that they were to be divided, not only in life, but also in death – i.e. as the result of Emma's death. Furthermore, Hardy implied that this was a punishment on him for his maltreatment of her:

I
I tore your letter into strips
No bigger than the airy feathers
That ducks preen out in changing weathers
Upon the shifting ripple-tips.

II
In darkness on my bed alone
I seemed to see you in a vision,

And hear you say: "Why this derision
Of one drawn to you, though unknown?"

VII
I learnt I had missed, by rash unheed,
My track; that, so the Will decided,
In life, death, we should be divided,
And at the sense I ached indeed.

VIII
That ache for you, born long ago,
Throbs on; I never could outgrow it.
What a revenge, did you but know it!
But that, thank God, you do not know.

In other words, Emma had got her own back for his derision of her.

17. Control

Kübler-Ross and Kessler described how the bereaved person attempts to take control of his or her life by becoming obsessional and controlling:

> 'but control feels empty and harsh as it covers up the more vulnerable sensations underneath. Control gives the illusion of safety and helps us think we are holding everything together, but an illusion is all it is.' In fact, 'trying to control the uncontrollable ultimately becomes a living hell, and grief has a way of amplifying everything and making people slaves to their own behavior.'[47]

Did Hardy become excessively controlling towards the household staff after the death of Emma? By all accounts, he was *already* excessively controlling towards them!

18. Fantasy

Kübler-Ross and Kessler gave the example of a lady called Beth and her mother, who:

> 'shared a fantasy about retirement. They made the plans and did the move; then her mother unexpectedly became ill. Now Beth

> lives with the fantasy of what might have been. Beth not only has the loss of her mother to grieve, but she also needs to separately, and simultaneously, mourn the fantasy.'[48]

Fantasy: the faculty or activity of imagining impossible or improbable things; a fanciful mental image, typically one on which a person often dwells, and which reflects their conscious or unconscious wishes.[49]

In his poem *The Coming of the End* (published in 1917), Hardy was shocked at the sudden death of Emma, when there was so much more to do and so much more to look forward to. But this was largely wishful thinking on Hardy's part, bearing in mind their virtual estrangement:

> I
> How it came to an end!
> The meeting afar from the crowd,
> And the love-looks and laughters unpenned,
> The parting when much was avowed,
> How it came to an end!
>
> II
> It came to an end;
> Yes, the outgazing over the stream,
> With the sun on each serpentine bend,
> Or, later, the luring moon-gleam;
> It came to an end.
>
> III
> It came to an end,
> The housebuilding, furnishing, planting,
> As if there were ages to spend
> In welcoming, feasting, and jaunting;
> It came to an end.

To Hardy's infinite regret, Emma died before the trees which he had planted around Max Gate to shelter the house from the wind and from prying eyes had fully grown. Hence his poem *Everything Comes* (published in 1917):

> 'The house is bleak and cold
> Built so new for me!
> All the winds upon the wold
> Search it through for me;

No screening trees abound,
And the curious eyes around
Keep on view for me.'

'My Love, I am planting trees
As a screen for you
Both from winds, and eyes that tease
And peer in for you.
Only wait till they have grown,
No such bower will be known
As I mean for you.'

'Then I will bear it, Love,
And will wait,' she said.
- So, with years, there grew a grove.
'Skill how great!' she said.
'As you wished, Dear?' – 'Yes, I see!
But – I'm dying; and for me
'Tis too late,' she said.

Wold: a piece of high, open, uncultivated land or moor.[50]

19. Strength

Kübler-Ross and Kessler posed the question, 'Why do people tell us to be strong?' Perhaps it was because:

> 'People are always more comfortable when the grieving person does not give off the sense that he or she is falling apart. If the grieving person doesn't cry and express too many emotions, we won't feel too much either. The truth is that pain can be contagious. You can't be around someone in deep sadness and not feel it, so if we put a lid on the grieving person's emotions, we won't have to deal with them ourselves.'
>
> 'But at what cost do we camouflage our grief? When we shelve our pain, it doesn't go away. Rather, it festers in a myriad of ways. We need to understand that strength and grief fit together. We must be strong to handle grief, and in the end, grief brings out the strengths we never knew we had.'[51]

Whether Florence urged Hardy to be strong is not known, but by her unswerving loyalty and devotion, she undoubtedly *made him stronger* than would otherwise have been the case. From where else did Hardy derive his strength? This will be discussed shortly.

In his poem '*Why do I*' (published in 1925), Hardy questioned whether he had the strength to go on, and he asked himself why he simply did not give up on living, for if he did, he could look forward to entering a realm where there would no longer be any pain:

> I
> Why do I go on doing these things?
> Why not cease?
> Is it that you are yet in this world of welterings
> And unease,
> And that, while so, mechanic repetitions please?

Welterings: turbulence.

20. Afterlife

Said Kübler-Ross and Kessler:

> 'Whatever the truth about life after death, we are certain that death does not exist as we imagine it. If you feel your loved one's presence, do not doubt it. They still exist. Birth is not a beginning and death is not an ending. They are merely points on a continuum [continuous sequence]. Death does not exist in its usually traditional form as an "ending to all". We are not suggesting that when you lose your loved one, you can skip the terrible pain of loss and separation, but we believe with all our hearts that even in death, our loved one still exists.'
>
> 'On the other hand, there are many in our society who believe that when you die, that is it. There is nothing else and your energy [i.e. your memory] lives on only in those around you.'[52]

In his poem entitled *Her Immortality* (published in 1898), Hardy referred to his 'dead Love' (Emma, of course), who told him that her immortality depended upon him staying alive:

> IX
> 'A Shade but in its mindful ones

Has immortality;
By living, me you keep alive,
By dying you slay me.

X
'In you resides my single power
Of sweet continuance here;
On your fidelity I count
Through many a coming year.'

To this, he replied:

XII
'I will not die, my One of all! -
To lengthen out thy days
I'll guard me from minutest harms
That may invest my ways!'

But he knew that one day he was bound to die, and then, as Emma lived on only in his memory so, in a sense, would she:

XIV
But grows my grief. When I surcease,
Through whom alone lives she,
Ceases my Love, her words, her ways,
Never again to be!

In the Spring of 1913, in his poem *Looking at a Picture on an Anniversary* (published in 1917), Hardy commemorated the 43rd anniversary of when he and Emma first met. He looked at her portrait, forever frozen at the time of her youth, and imagined that she recognized him. A portrait of Emma Lavinia Gifford aged thirty by an unknown artist was donated to the Dorset County Museum by Emma's nephew Gordon Gifford in 1949. Perhaps this was the one that Hardy had in mind?

And surely this most important date must serve to revitalize Emma, he thought; surely it meant that her consciousness/spirit lived on, even though physically, she was no more? And if not, then his own life was meaningless to him:

But don't you know it, my dear,
Don't you know it,
That this day of the year
(What rainbow-rays embow it!)

We met, strangers confessed,
But parted-blest?

Though at this query, my dear,
There in your frame
Unmoved you still appear,
You must be thinking the same,
But keep that look demure
Just to allure.

And now at length a trace
I surely vision
Upon that wistful face
Of old-time recognition,
Smiling forth, 'Yes, as you say,
It is the day.'

For this one phase of you
Now left on earth
This great date must endue
With pulsings of rebirth? -
I see them vitalize
Those two deep eyes!

But if this face I con
Does not declare
Consciousness living on
Still in it, little I care
To live myself, my dear,
Lone-labouring here!

'I con': presumably 'I am conscious of'.

Endue: endow with or provide with a quality or ability.[53]

So here is Hardy, whose intellect tells him that there is no logical reason to believe in immortality, unable to bear the thought that Emma is no longer with him, even in spirit, and unable to see the point of going on, if this is the case.

Spirit: the non-physical part of a person which is the seat of emotions and character; the soul. Such a part is regarded as a person's true self and capable of surviving physical death or separation.[54]

In his aforementioned poem '*Why Do I*' (published in 1925), Hardy hinted, once again, that despite his scepticism in regard to the Christian religion, he believed in the immortality of the soul.

> II
> When shall I leave off doing these things? —
> When I hear
> You have dropped your dusty cloak and taken you wondrous
>   wings
> To another sphere,
> Where no pain is: Then shall I hush this dinning gear.

Din: a loud, unpleasant, and prolonged noise.[55]

Given the fact that Hardy's mind was in turmoil after the death of Emma, and given that this turmoil persisted, it is understandable that he vacillated between believing in some sort of afterlife, and therefore hopefully a reunion with Emma, and rejecting such a concept altogether.

Chapter 6

Hardy and the Inner World of Grief: Hauntings

To haunt, in this context, means to be persistently and disturbingly present in the mind.[1] Kübler-Ross and Kessler gave the example of a lady called Joyce, who:

> 'was walking down Market Street in San Francisco about three months after her close friend Michael had died. She was surprised when she spotted a man she thought could easily have been Michael, with the same hair and body type. Even his walk was the same.' This, the authors described as a 'Visual Haunting'. The authors continued:
>
> 'There are many types of hauntings, such as sounds you hear, people you see, words with echo, and even the physical sensation of being touched. You may be tormented by a scene you wish you hadn't witnessed, like a loved one with tubes sticking out of everywhere, the smell of the hospital room, or the pained expression on your loved one's face. Maybe you can't shape the way she looked when she was diagnosed. Or when she was dying. Or after she died. Whatever it is, the loved one is gone but the visions remain.'[2]

That Hardy was haunted by memories of Emma after her death is attested to by the numerous poems he wrote on this theme. Hardy's poem *The Going* (composed in December 1912, the month after Emma's death, and published in 1914), contains elements not only of hauntings, but also of regrets and loss. He revealed how the sudden and unexpected death of Emma had come as the most tremendous shock to him. He also described experiencing a hallucination in that, for an instant, he believed that he saw her subsequently.

Hallucinate: to experience a seemingly real perception of something not actually present.[3]

He recalled how, when they had first met, Emma rode her pony along Beeny cliff top. He also recalled, sadly, how in the later years of their marriage, there was a silence between them. He admitted that it was now too late to put matters right. Finally, he declared that Emma would never know how her death would 'undo' him. In other words, Emma would never bear witness to his profound anguish and dismay:

> Why did you give no hint that night
> That quickly after the morrow's dawn,
> And calmly, as if indifferent quite,
> You would close your term here, up and be gone
> Where I could not follow
> With wing of swallow
> To gain one glimpse of you ever anon!
>
> Never to bid good-bye
> Or lip me the softest call,
> Or utter a wish for a word, while I
> Saw morning harden upon the wall,
> Unmoved, unknowing
> That your great going
> Had place that moment, and altered all.
>
> Why do you make me leave the house
> And think for a breath it is you I see
> At the end of the alley of bending boughs
> Where so often at dusk you used to be;
> Till in darkening dankness
> The yawning blankness
> Of the perspective sickens me!
>
> You were she who abode
> By those red-veined rocks far West,
> You were the swan-necked one who rode
> Along the beetling Beeny Crest,
> And, reining nigh me,
> Would muse and eye me,
> While Life unrolled us its very best.

How happy Hardy had been, in those heady days!

> Why, then, latterly did we not speak,
> Did we not think of those days long dead,
> And ere your vanishing strive to seek

That time's renewal? We might have said,
'In this bright spring weather
We'll visit together
Those places that once we visited.'

How Hardy so regretted that he and Emma had not been given the opportunity, prior to her death, to rekindle the love that they had once shared!

Well, well! All's past amend,
Unchangeable. It must go.
I seem but a dead man held on end
To sink down soon .... O you could not know
That such swift fleeing
No soul foreseeing -
Not even I - would undo me so!

In his poignant poem *The Voice* (composed in December 1912, the month after Emma's death, and published in 1914), Hardy imagined that he heard the voice of his late and dearly beloved Emma, as she was when he first met her and not as she was latterly, when their attitude towards each other had changed for the worst. He struggled to accept the fact that he would never see her physique or hear her voice again, and he knew that without her, he would find it desperately difficult to continue with his own life:

Woman much missed, how you call to me, call to me,
Saying that now you are not as you were
When you had changed from the one who was all to me,
But as at first, when our day was fair.

Can it be you that I hear? Let me view you, then,
Standing as when I drew near to the town
Where you would wait for me: yes, as I knew you then,
Even to the original air-blue gown!

Or is it only the breeze, in its listlessness
Travelling across the wet mead to me here,
You being ever dissolved to wan wistlessness,
Heard no more again far or near?

Thus I; faltering forward,
Leaves around me falling,
Wind oozing thin through the thorn from norward,
And the woman calling.

Wan: pale, and giving the impression of illness or exhaustion.[4]

In his poem *The Shadow on the Stone* (commenced in 1913, completed in 1916, and published in 1917), Hardy had the illusion that Emma was present, and yet he dared not confront the illusion for fear of discovering that *it was just that* - an illusion!

Illusion: a false idea or belief.[5]

> I went by the Druid stone
> That broods in the garden white and lone,
> And I stopped and looked at the shifting shadows
> That at some moments fall thereon
> From the tree hard by with a rhythmic swing,
> And they shaped in my imagining
> To the shade that a well-known head and shoulders
> Threw there when she was gardening.
>
> I thought her behind my back,
> Yea, her I long had learned to lack,
> And I said: 'I am sure you are standing behind me,
> Though how do you get into this old track?'
> And there was no sound but the fall of a leaf
> As a sad response; and to keep down grief
> I would not turn my head to discover
> That there was nothing in my belief.
>
> Yet I wanted to look and see
> That nobody stood at the back of me;
> But I thought once more: 'Nay, I'll not unvision
> A shape which, somehow, there may be.'
> So I went on softly from the glade,
> And left her behind me throwing her shade,
> As she were indeed an apparition —
> My head unturned lest my dream should fade.

Druid stone: one of a number of standing stones from the Neolithic period (4,000-3001 BCE) located in the grounds of Max Gate.

In his poem *The Phantom Horsewoman* (published in 1914), Hardy revealed that, indelibly imprinted in his mind, was the magical time when he first met Emma. She would henceforth be forever in his thoughts, and that memory of her was forever frozen in time, especially of her riding her pony on the coast of North Cornwall:

> Queer are the ways of a man I know:
> He comes and stands
> In a careworn craze,
> And looks at the sands
> And the seaward haze
> With moveless hands
> And face and gaze,
> Then turns to go…
> And what does he see when he gazes so?
>
> They say he sees as an instant thing
> More clear than to-day,
> A sweet soft scene
> That once was in play
> By that briny green;
> Yes, notes alway
> Warm, real, and keen,
> What his back years bring —
> A phantom of his own figuring.

Of this vision of his they might say more:
Not only there
Does he see this sight,
But everywhere
In his brain—day, night,
As if on the air
It were drawn rose-bright —
Yea, far from that shore

Does he carry this vision of heretofore:

> A ghost-girl-rider. And though, toil-tried,
> He withers daily,
> Time touches her not,
> But she still rides gaily
> In his rapt thought
> On that shagged and shaly
> Atlantic spot,
> And as when first eyed

Draws rein and sings to the swing of the tide.

To experience a 'flashback' is to focus one's mind on or vividly remember a past time or incident.[6] Here Hardy is describing a scene from the distant past as if it is recurring in the present time, featuring Emma whom he looks back on with love and wonder, not to say adoration. Not all flashbacks are pleasant, however, as will be seen.

In his poem *At Castle Boterel* (published in 1914), Hardy again saw his late wife Emma as 'a phantom figure':

I
As I drive to the junction of lane and highway,
And the drizzle bedrenches the waggonette,
I look behind at the fading byway,
And see on its slope, now glistening wet,
Distinctly yet

II
Myself and a girlish form benighted
In dry March weather. We climb the road
Beside a chaise. We had just alighted
To ease the sturdy pony's load
When he sighed and slowed.

III
What we did as we climbed, and what we talked of
Matters not much, nor to what it led, -
Something that life will not be balked of
Without rude reason till hope is dead,
And feeling fled.

VI
And to me, though Time's unflinching rigour,
In mindless rote, has ruled from sight
The substance now, one phantom figure
Remains on the slope, as when that night
Saw us alight.

VII
I look and see it there, shrinking, shrinking,
I look back at it amid the rain
For the very last time; for my sand is sinking,

And I shall traverse old love's domain
Never again.

'Castle Boterel': Hardy's name for Boscastle.

In his poem *The Woman I met* (published in 1922), Hardy found himself having troublesome thoughts about his late wife Emma, who he felt in a sense was still with him. Emma had tortured him, he affirmed, even though he had worshipped her, and 'heaven' determined that this was the cross that he must bear. Finally, he alluded to the fact that although he had loved Emma, he believed that during the marriage, she had despised and tormented him:

I
A stranger, I threaded sunken-hearted
A lamp-lit crowd;
And anon there passed me a soul departed,
Who mutely bowed.
In my far-off youthful years I had met her,
Full-pulsed; but now, no more life's debtor,
Onward she slid
In a shroud that furs half-hid.

II
'Why do you trouble me, dead woman,
Trouble me;
You whom I knew when warm and human?
How it be
That you quitted earth and are yet upon it
Is, to any who ponder on it,
Past being read!'
'Still, it is so,' she said.

IV
'Well; your very simplicity made me love you
Mid such town dross,
Till I set not Heaven itself above you,
Who grew my Cross;
For you'd only nod, despite how I sighed for you;
So you tortured me, who fain would have died for you!
—What I suffered then
Would have paid for the sins of ten!

V
'Thus went the days. I feared you despised me
To fling me a nod
Each time, no more: till love chastised me
As with a rod
That a fresh bland boy of no assurance
Should fire me with passion beyond endurance,
While others all
I hated, and loathed their call.

Chapter 7

Thomas Hardy and the Outer World of Grief

In their book *On Grief and Grieving*, under the heading 'The Outer World of Grief', Kübler-Ross and Kessler included the following subheadings.

1. Anniversaries

Said Kübler-Ross and Kessler:

> 'We don't realize how many anniversaries there are in life until after a loss. We are aware that there will be anniversaries of the day our loved one died, but we forget the celebrations and/or remembrances of birth, marriages, that first date, and the millions of things in between. Whatever happiness they once brought, they now bring memories of deep loss. Every symbol of the anniversary of the death matters to us: the one-month anniversary, six months, a year. Joy is replaced on those days now by the feeling of loss.'[1]

No one was more assiduous in commemorating anniversaries than Hardy, in particular that relating to the late Emma. For example, on 27 November 1922 he wrote:

> 'E's [Emma's] Death day, ten years ago. Went with F. [Florence] and tidied her tomb and carry flowers for her and the other two tombs [i.e. those of his parents Thomas and Jemima and his siblings Mary and Henry].'[2]

On 7 March 1924, Hardy wrote:

> 'E. first met 54 years ago' – in other words, he had met Emma on that date in 1870. And 'Mother died 20 years ago today'.[3]

2. Sex

Said Kübler-Ross and Kessler:

> 'Sex is a part of life, so it is also a part of grief. When a husband or wife or lover dies, there is a loss of sex as well. You may have wonderful memories of lovemaking, which are not so easily discussed with friends. Maybe you want to have sex right away, and maybe you'll never want it again as long as you live. One thing is for sure: if sex is part of the relationship, it will be part of the grief.'[4]

However, as already mentioned, sex evidently featured little or not at all in Hardy's relationship with Emma.

3. Your Body and Your Health

Kübler-Ross and Kessler gave the example of a person called Byron and his wife Donna:

> 'When Byron died, Donna was in a shocking haggard state. She did her best to look good but even after she was freshly showered, with hair and makeup in place, everyone talked about how this loss had added ten years to Donna.'[5]

Whether the death of Emma caused Hardy to age prematurely is not known. However, he had no notion that, in his own words, her death 'would undo me so'.

Undo: cause the downfall or ruin of.[6]

4. So Much to Do

Said Kübler-Ross and Kessler insightfully:

> After a bereavement, 'there is so much to do: make the calls, make the plans, make the arrangements.[7]

Hardy, of course, had servants to help him, and most importantly the loyal and dutiful Florence who, said Flower, 'arranged the funeral' and 'took all responsibilities upon herself' before returning to London.[8]

5. Clothes and Possessions

Said Kübler-Ross and Kessler:

> 'While there is so much going on inside of you, a myriad of tasks await outside. One of these tasks is to pack up your loved one's clothing. Another is to decide what to do with it. This often feels like the most difficult job of all because to deal with a person's possessions is to clearly face the fact that they are gone. If they were still here, we would not be going through their things - it would be an intrusion on their privacy. The bottom line is that glasses, shoes, and coats force our acceptance of a harsh reality.'[9]

People react in various ways when they lose a loved one, in respect of that loved one's possessions. Some cannot bear to see them because this reinforces the anguish of what has been lost. This is especially true of photographs. Others find them to be a comfort. What of Emma's possessions? Did Hardy retain them, or did he dispose of them?

Hardy's sketch of Emma entitled 'Searching for the Glass', made by him during their early courting days and dated 1870, which was presumably in his possession, survived. Similarly, Emma's *Diaries* and *Some Recollections* also survived.

Two copies of Emma's book *Spaces*, described by writer, biographer, radio producer, playwright, and poet Robert Gittings as 'an apocalyptic prose vision' were also to be found in Hardy's library after her death. 'In her description of the Day of Judgment', said Gittings, Emma wrote:

> 'Peoples of the world everywhere will prostrate themselves, the electric lights of the world will shine forth again, not *lit* by mortal hands which will have failed to set them aglow .... They will gleam and burn fiercely with an awful intensity toward their final burning up of the earth ....'[10]

This is described as 'religiosity' on Emma's part: religiose being defined as being excessively religious.[11]

Several photographs of Emma also survived, not having been disposed of by Hardy. Finally, Hardy's library contained three copies of the *Holy Bible*, one of which presumably was the aforementioned one presented to him by Emma.

However, Hardy did destroy the two aforementioned books written by Emma, entitled: *The Pleasures of Heaven and the Pains of Hell*, and *What*

I Think of My Husband which, according to Florence, contained 'the core of their tragedy'. Had these documents survived, this would have made it possible for Emma's views about Hardy to be more fully understood.

In Dorchester auctioneer Henry Duke's, catalogue of the sale of Max Gate's 'Furniture, Paintings, Prints, and Other Effects' on 16 February 1938, nothing else relating to Emma appears.

In his poem *A Circular*, composed in 1913, the year following Emma's death, (and published in 1914), Hardy described himself reading an advertisement for ladies' clothes, possibly one sent to Max Gate by a clothing manufacturer who was unaware of Emma's death:

> As 'legal representative'
> I read a missive not my own,
> On new designs the senders give
> For clothes, in tints as shown.
>
> Here figure blouses, gowns for tea,
> And presentation-trains of state,
> Charming ball-dresses, millinery,
> Warranted up to date.
>
> And this gay-pictured, spring-time shout
> Of Fashion, hails what lady proud?
> Her who before last year was out
> Was costumed in a shroud.

6. Holidays

In respect of holidays, said Kübler-Ross and Kessler:

> 'How can you celebrate togetherness when there is none? When you have lost someone special, your world loses it celebratory qualities. Holidays only magnify the loss. The sadness feels sadder, and the loneliness goes deeper. The need for support may be the greatest during the holidays.'[12]

Whether Hardy regarded excursions to favourite places that he had shared with Emma as holidays is debatable, but at least he had the company of Florence, or his brother Henry or his sister Kate, on these excursions/ pilgrimages.

7. Letter writing

Said Kübler-Ross and Kessler:

> 'Grief must be externalized. Our pain and sadness can be fully realized only when we release them. For many, writing letters to their loved one is a convenient, always available way to get the words out and communicate.' But 'What - or even why - should you write to someone with whom communication seems to be lost?'[13]
>
> 'Writing is a wonderful companion to our loneliness in a world where we stand alone. Many people write about their feelings after a loss. Some write in a grief journal to deposit their feelings without worrying about someone else's reactions. For many, writing feels better than speaking, as the unspoken healing can come through journaling. You can find your voice in writing in a way that you can't find in other forms of communication.'
>
> 'We are filled with so many memories, feelings, hopes, dreams, stories, insights, reactions, and questions that are all wanting to get out and take their rightful place. The written word can be their expression.'[14]

Hardy was a prolific letter writer, and his collected letters fill 8 volumes. After Emma's death, he revealed his feelings to several of his correspondents, as will be seen and, perhaps by doing so this served as a catharsis for him. Also, he may have felt relieved and thankful to have trusted relatives and friends with whom to share his sorrow.

Catharsis: the process of releasing, and thereby providing relief from, strong or repressed emotions.[15]

8. Age

Said Kübler-Ross and Kessler:

> 'For you as the one left behind, your age is also a factor. There is no denying that, for the most part, the longer we've lived the more experience with loss we have had. Of course, there are many exceptions, but more years in the world also provides us with deeper experiences of support systems, problem solving,

> and emotional maturity, things we didn't have in place when we were younger.'[16]
>
> 'An older person in retirement may have more time to think about the loss. They may feel less need to rejoin the world, thinking that they have already seen and done enough. This may lead to depression in many cases, while in others it can result in more contentment with what is left.'[17]

Hardy was aged 71 when Emma died and yes, he had already suffered the loss of his parents, Thomas in 1892 and Jemima in 1904. However, the loss of a partner is of a different dimension, not least on account of the 'love hormones' which are involved, as will be seen.

9. Closure

Said Kübler-Ross and Kessler:

> 'No matter how you work at feeling your feelings fully, you never really find the closure that you hear about or see in movies. But you do find a place for loss, a way to hold it and live with it.'
>
> 'In grieving we mistakenly think we can finish everything, but grief is not a project with a beginning and an end. It is a reflection of a loss that never goes away. We simply learn to live with it, both in the foreground and in the background. You don't ever bring the grief over a loved one to a close.'[18]

This is profoundly true for anyone who has ever truly loved and it was absolutely true of Hardy, as his poems and writings reveal. For instance, in his poem *A Leaving* (published in 1925), he revealed how the day of Emma's funeral, and every moment of that day, was seared forever into his memory:

> Knowing what it bore
> I watched the rain-smitten back of the car—
> (Brown-curtained, such as the old ones were)—
> When it started forth for a journey afar
> Into the sullen November air,
> And passed the glistening laurels and round the bend.
>
> I have seen many gayer vehicles turn that bend
> In autumn, winter, and summer air,
> Bearing for journeys near or afar

Many who now are not, but were,
But I don't forget that rain-smitten car,
Knowing what it bore!

When Hardy said, 'I don't forget', that indicates that he was experiencing flashbacks of a disturbing nature. Continued the authors:

> 'It's common for people who've experienced very upsetting or traumatic experiences to have "flashbacks" about what happened to them. Flashbacks are very powerful memories which feel very real and can be very distressing. A survivor may feel like the traumatic event is taking place again and may even be able to smell scents, hear sounds or feel pain that they experienced at the time.'
>
> 'When someone experiences a distressing experience the mechanism for processing memories can become overwhelmed. This means the mind is not able to process the experience in the usual way and the memory remains active. The memory can easily be triggered by anything that reminds the person of what happened such as a place, person, smell, or sound. People who've experienced traumatic experiences may also "relive" what happened in nightmares.'[19]

Hardy was not only present at Emma's funeral, he was also present at her death, and the vision of her dying in her attic room at Max Gate would undoubtedly have recurred over and over again in his mind as a flashback. Anyone who has lost a beloved partner will know just how traumatic this experience can be. And from his poems, reading between the lines, it is more than likely that Hardy, with his renowned attention to detail, would have had flashbacks about innumerable aspects of Emma's life, and the times spent with her. Today, of course, specialist counselling is on offer to those who experience distressing flashbacks of this nature: sadly, not so in Hardy's day.

If Hardy continued to mourn the loss of Emma until the day he died, as the evidence seems to indicate, then this indicates a little discussed aspect of the five stages of grief, namely that it is possible either to remain static in this regard, or even to regress. Hardy, instead of moving forward through the aforementioned stages of grief towards acceptance, remained, for the most part, in one or other of the earlier stages: of denial; anger; bargaining; depression.

Chapter 8

When Death is Sudden and Unexpected

Under this heading, Kübler-Ross and Kessler stated as follows:

> 'Death is hardest to comprehend without any forewarning. The news and loss are crushing. How can our world change so dramatically and without any warning? No preparation, no goodbyes, just the loudest absence one could ever imagine. As a result, in sudden death, the denial will be longer and deeper.' This certainly seems to have been the case with Hardy.
>
> 'The suddenness thrusts us into a new, abnormal world. How can you grasp that your loved one was here for breakfast and dead by lunchtime? You can't.'[1]
>
> 'You don't grieve, because you can't yet. You are in free fall, with your grief deeply buried under your shock, trauma, and pain. It will stay there for you gradually to unearth it over several years.'
>
> 'For some, the more sudden the death, the longer it will take to grieve the loss. The period of denial is substantially lengthened, with no chance to say goodbye and to adjust to a life without your nearest and dearest.[2] The sudden loss of a loved one is a particular kind of death. The sorrow of not saying goodbye hurts the most when we lose someone in the midst of a life. We wonder how it could have happened, and what we might have done to change the outcome.'[3]

Writing on 17 July 2004, Elisabeth Kübler-Ross described grief in her own life:

> 'I am no stranger to grief, although few people have actually seen me grieving. While I have made a career of dealing with death and dying, I came to my grief late in life. Having spent the last nine years partially paralysed due to my strokes, I have often

> felt purposeless, even though I know I am still here for a reason. During this time, I've had the opportunity to write two more books with my co-writer [David Kessler].'[4] This was a reference to *Life's Lesson*, and *On Grief and Grieving* (published in 2001 and 2005 respectively).

The fact that Elisabeth had experienced grief herself lends to her books a profound and unique authenticity.

On 27 November 1912, the very day of Emma's death, Hardy wrote to Charles Edwin Gifford, retired Paymaster-in-Chief of the Royal Navy and Emma's first cousin, to say:

> 'You will be grieved and shocked to hear that Emma died this morning shortly after nine o'clock. Her illness has been quite a slight one, & she was downstairs at tea on Monday evening. I was with her, fortunately, when she breathed her last. I am too distressed to write more. The funeral is fixed for Saturday at 2.30 at Stinsford Church, two miles from here. We leave this house about 1.45.'[5]

On 29 November 1912, Hardy wrote as follows to the Reverend Alfred Metcalfe, rector of St Peter's Church, Dorchester:

> 'As my wife was so frequently a member of your congregation and in such accord with your views, I have thought that if you would *like* to take part in the funeral service at Stinsford tomorrow with Mr Cowley I should be much pleased.'[6] This was a reference to the Reverend H. G. B. Cowley, Vicar of Stinsford.

On 17 December 1912, in a letter to Florence Henniker (née Milnes), Hardy elaborated further on the events immediately leading up to Emma's demise. Said he:

> 'Emma's death was absolutely unexpected by me, the doctor, & everybody, though not sudden, strictly speaking. She was quite well a week before, & (as I fancy) in an unlucky moment determined to motor to some friends about 6 miles off. During the night following she had a bad attack of indigestion, which I attributed to the jolting of the car. She was never well from that time, though she came down to tea with some callers on the Monday evening before her death on Wednesday morning. I was with her when she passed away. Half an hour earlier she had told

> the servant that she felt better. Then her bell rang violently, & when we went up she was gasping. In five minutes all was over.'[7]

Likewise on 21 December 1912, to aristocrat and writer Lady Agnes Grove (née Fox), Hardy wrote of Emma:

> 'About a week before her death she went for a motor drive, & the night following had violent dyspepsia. She continued unwell, more or less, from this, but two days before the end, came down to tea with some Americans who called, & she seemed better. She would not see a doctor till the evening before her death, & he merely treated her for weakness arising from her having been able to assimilate no food for several days. The next morning a sudden gasping came on & before the doctor could reach the house she was gone. Heart failure from some internal perforation he called it - which implies that mischief had been working for some while. Yet I never had a suspicion but that her constitution was quite sound.'
>
> 'A doctor' was a reference to Dr B. W. N. Gowring, who gave the cause of death as 'Impacted Gallstones' and 'Heart Failure'.[8]

On 26 December 1912 to barrister and politician Sir Robert Pearce Edgcumbe, Hardy wrote:

> 'To thank you sincerely for your kind words of sympathy with me in my loss. It was so unforeseen that I can scarcely realize it at times even now, my impression having been for many years that she would be with me till I departed. I feel a great blank to have come over [my] life by this.'[9]

Curiously enough, it seems never to have occurred to Hardy that Emma would die and leave him. This is apparent in his poem *Best Times* (published in 1922), in which he recalled Emma and her beauty, and happy times spent in her company, never imagining that one evening, when she went upstairs to bed, that this would be the last time.

> 'Best Times'
>
> We went a day's excursion to the stream,
> Basked by the bank, and bent to the ripple-gleam,
> And I did not know
> That life would show,
> However it might flower, no finer glow.

Thomas Hardy and the Death of Emma

I walked in the Sunday sunshine by the road
That wound towards the wicket of your abode,
And I did not think
That life would shrink
To nothing ere it shed a rosier pink.

Unlooked for I arrived on a rainy night,
And you hailed me at the door by the swaying light,
And I full forgot
That life might not
Again be touching that ecstatic height.

And that calm eve when you walked up the stair,
After a gaiety prolonged and rare,
No thought soever
That you might never
Walk down again, struck me as I stood there.

After the death of Emma, Hardy kept his perpetual desk calendar set to the date when he first met her.

Chapter 9

Thomas Hardy's Personal Experience of Bereavement

Everyone is different, each person grieves in their own unique way, and Hardy was no exception. Furthermore, the stages of grief are more nuanced than Kübler-Ross and Kessler have indicated in their book *On Grief and Grieving*. This is not surprising, as no one volume could possibly cover all aspects of the subject. In summary, no list of the emotions experienced by a bereaved person can be fully comprehensive. However, some additional ones peculiar to Hardy are now put forward.

1. Hardy Believed that *Only He* Remembered Emma

In his poem *Places*, composed in March 1913, the year after Emma's death, Hardy bewailed the fact that nobody now remembered her birth in Plymouth, Devonshire, or her riding her pony at 'Boterel' (Boscastle).

> Nobody says: Ah, that is the place
> Where chanced, in the hollow of years ago,
> What none of the Three Towns cared to know -
> The birth of a little girl of grace -
> The sweetest the house saw, first or last;
> Yet it was so
> On that day long past.
>
> Nobody thinks: There, there she lay
> In a room by the Hoe, like the bud of a flower,
> And listened, just after the bedtime hour,
> To the stammering chimes that used to play
> The quaint Old Hundred-and-Thirteenth tune
> In Saint Andrew's tower
> Night, morn, and noon.

Nobody calls to mind that here
Upon Boterel Hill, where the carters skid,
With cheeks whose airy flush outbid
Fresh fruit in bloom, and free of fear,
She cantered down, as if she must fall
(Though she never did),
To the charm of all.

Nay: one there is to whom these things,
That nobody else's mind calls back,
Have a savour that scenes in being lack,
And a presence more than the actual brings;
To whom to-day is beneaped and stale,
And its urgent clack
But a vapid tale.

Three Towns: Plymouth, Devonport, and East Stonehouse which were formerly merged, in 1914, to become the Borough of Plymouth.

Hoe: Plymouth Hoe, a promenade offering panoramic views over Plymouth Sound.

Saint Andrew's tower: of Plymouth's Minster Church of St Andrew.

In his poem '*You were the Sort that Men Forget*' (published in 1917), Hardy alluded to the fact that, to his great regret, Emma did not get on with other people, and could be tactless, offensive, artless, and lacking in empathy. But despite all, he held her lovingly in his memory, and again believed himself to be the only one who did so.

I
You were the sort that men forget;
Though I - not yet! -
Perhaps not ever. Your slighted weakness
Adds to the strength of my regret!

II
You'd not the art - you never had
For good or bad -
To make men see how sweet your meaning,
Which, visible, had charmed them glad.

III
You would, by words inept let fall,
Offend them all,

Even if they saw your warm devotion
Would hold your life's blood at their call.

V
I am now the only being who
Remembers you
It may be. What a waste that Nature
Grudged soul so dear the art its due!

To Florence Henniker on 28 December 1918, Hardy wrote:

> 'As it is an exceptionally mild afternoon, I have been gardening a little, & had to tie up a rosebush planted by Emma a month or two before her death: it has grown luxuriantly, & she would be pleased if she could know & that I care for it.'[1]

This letter indicates that Emma was ostensibly in good health not long before her untimely death. Also, that after her death, Hardy cherished her memory.

2. How Hardy Revisited the Happy Scenes of his Courting Days

In his grief, Hardy looked back to the past. To Edward Clodd on 13 December 1912, Hardy wrote thus of himself and Emma:

> 'One forgets all the recent years & differences, & the mind goes back to the early times when each was much to the other - in her case & mine intensely much.'[2]

After Emma's death, Hardy evidently found solace in revisiting places associated with his late wife, and in particular St Juliot, where he and she had first met, and its environs. On 6 March 1913, said Florence, which was:

> 'forty-three years ... almost to a day, after his first journey to Cornwall, he started for St. Juliot, putting up at Boscastle, and visiting Pentargan Bay and Beeny Cliff, on which he had not once set foot in the long interval. He found the rectory and other scenes with which he had been so familiar changed a little, but not greatly, and returning by way of Plymouth arranged for a memorial tablet to Mrs Hardy in the church with which she had been so closely associated as organist before her marriage, and in

other ways. The tablet was afterwards erected to his own design, as was also the tomb in Stinsford Churchyard - in the preparation of which memorials he had to revive a species [kind] of work that he had been unaccustomed to since the years of his architectural pupilage.'[3]

3. Hardy's Endless but Fruitless Search for Emma: the Pain of Remembrance

In his poem *The Glimpse* (published in 1917), Hardy searched endlessly but in vain for his beautiful late wife Emma, and imagined he saw and heard her. But this, of course, was an illusion:

She sped through the door
And, following in haste,
And stirred to the core,
I entered hot-faced;
But I could not find her,
No sign was behind her.
'Where is she?' I said:
- 'Who?' they asked that sat there;
'Not a soul's come in sight.'
- 'A maid with red hair.'
- 'Ah.' They paled. 'She is dead ….
People see her at night,
But you are the first
On whom she has burst
In the keen common light.'

It was ages ago,
When I was quite strong:
I have waited since, - O,
I have waited so long!
- Yea, I set me to own
The house, where now lone
I dwell in void rooms
Booming hollow as tombs!
But I never come near her,
Though nightly I hear her.
And my cheek has grown thin
And my hair has grown gray

With this waiting therein;
But she still keeps away!

So, despite having the love and companionship of Florence, his wife of 3 years, Hardy continued to feel anguished and lonely 4 years after the death of Emma.

In his poem *They would not Come* (published in 1922), Hardy described a visit to a place where Emma had once prayed and to where a friend of his had once preached (probably Plymouth where Emma had been brought up), but her voice was absent and all that greeted him was silence. Here, and elsewhere, Hardy evokes the pain of loss as poignantly and dramatically as any other writer:

I
I travelled to where in her lifetime
She'd knelt at morning prayer,
To call her up as if there;
But she paid no heed to my suing,
As though her old haunt could win not
A thought from her spirit, or care.

II
I went where my friend had lectioned
The prophets in high declaim,
That my soul's ear the same
Full tones should catch as aforetime;
But silenced by gear of the Present
Was the voice that once there came!

Sue: appeal formally to a person for something.[4]

Lection: reading of a text found in a particular copy or edition.[5]

In his poem *A Gentleman's Epitaph on Himself and a Lady, who were Buried Together* (published in 1922), Hardy provided several clues that this poem, like so many others, related to himself and Emma. For example, where they both lived, and the colour of her eyes, which were famously blue!

I
I dwelt in the shade of a city,
She far by the sea,
With folk perhaps good, gracious, witty;
But never with me.

IV
Maybe she had eyes of deep colour,
Maybe they were blue,
Maybe as she aged they got duller;
That never I knew.

But the final two verses indicate that, if the poem *does relate to Hardy and Emma*, then theirs *was always a loveless marriage*:

VI
Not a word passed of love all our lifetime,
Between us, nor thrill;
We'd never a husband-and-wife time,
For good or for ill.

VII
Yet as one dust, through bleak days and vernal,
Lie I and lies she,
This never-known lady, eternal
Companion to me!

4. Hardy's Tendency to have Morbid Thoughts

Hardy's poem *Looking Across* (composed in December 1915 and published in 1917) indicates that he was thinking of four members of his family who had been buried at Stinsford, and that he was asking himself, why had he not joined them and what was the point of going on himself? The four were his parents Thomas and Jemima, his late wife Emma, and his sister Mary:

It is dark in the sky,
And silence is where
Our laughs rang high;
And recall do I
That One is out there.

The dawn is not nigh,
And the trees are bare,
And the waterways sigh
That a year has drawn by,
And Two are out there.

The wind drops to die
Like the phantom of Care
Too frail for a cry,
And heart brings to eye
That Three are out there.

This Life runs dry
That once ran rare
And rosy in dye,
And fleet the days fly,
And Four are out there.

Tired, tired am I
Of this earthly air,
And my wraith asks: Why,
Since these calm lie,
Are not Five out there?

In other words, Hardy believed that he would only be at peace when his earthly life came to an end.

In his poem *When Dead* (published in 1925), Hardy affirmed that he would prefer it if his life were to end, when he would be entombed in the churchyard, beneath the trees. Also, despite his lack of faith, he believed that then, he and Emma would be reunited, and he would be more considerate to her in death than he had been in life:

I
It will be much better when
I am under the bough;
I shall be more myself, Dear, then,
Than I am now.

II
No sign of querulousness
To wear you out
Shall I show there: strivings and stress
Be quite without.

IV
And when you come to me
To show you true.

Doubt not I shall infallibly
Be waiting you.

Under the bough: i.e. buried beneath the bough of a churchyard tree.

Querulousness: here Hardy appears to admit that he could be querulous – defined as complaining in a rather petulant or whining manner.[6]

Here, once again, Hardy indicated that *he did* believe in an afterlife.

5. Hardy's Bewilderment

In his song entitled *The Rift* (published in 1922), Hardy indicated that he had no idea what he had done wrong, in respect of his marriage to Emma:

'Twas just at gnat and cobweb-time,
When yellow begins to show in the leaf,
That your old gamut changed its chime
From those true tones — of span so brief! —
That met my beats of joy, of grief,
As rhyme meets rhyme.

So sank I from my high sublime!
We faced but chancewise after that,
And never I knew or guessed my crime. …
Yes; 'twas the date — or nigh thereat —
Of the yellowing leaf; at moth and gnat
And cobweb-time.

This is quite plausible, in that although Hardy was undoubtedly neglectful of Emma's welfare in the later years of their marriage, her personality disorder, and her consequent disdainful criticism of him, was without doubt the fundamental cause of their rift.

6. How Hardy regretted the fact that Emma, as a deceased person, could no longer experience what had given her joy during her time on earth

In his poem *Lament* (published in 1914), Hardy recalled those activities, pleasures, and joys in which the late Emma would have delighted, had she lived, and he rued the fact that she was no longer alive and able to do so.

I
How she would have loved
A party to-day! -
Bright-hatted and gloved,
With table and tray
And chairs on the lawn
Her smiles would have shone
With welcomings.... But
She is shut, she is shut
From friendship's spell
In the jailing shell
Of her tiny cell.

III
And she would have sought
With a child's eager glance
The shy snowdrops brought
By the new year's advance,
And peered in the rime
Of Candlemas-time
For crocuses... chanced
It that she were not tranced
From sights she loved best;
Wholly possessed
By an infinite rest!

IV
And we are here staying
Amid these stale things
Who care not for gaying,
And those junketings
That wed so to joy her,
And never to cloy her
As us they cloy!... But
She is shut, she is shut
From the cheer of them, dead
To all done and said
In a yew-arched bed.

Candlemas: a Christian festival held on 2 February to commemorate the purification of the Virgin Mary and the presentation of Christ in the Temple. Candles were traditionally blessed in this festival.[7]

Rime: frost.[8]

Trance: a half-conscious state characterized by an absence of response to external stimuli.[9]

Junket: an extravagant trip or celebration.[10]

Cloy: disgust or sicken with an excess of sweetness, richness, or sentiment.[11]

7. How Hardy Longed to Put Back the Clock

In his song '*If it's ever Spring again*' (published in 1922), Hardy exhibited a longing to turn back the clock, and to retrace the steps he had once taken with Emma by his side:

> If it's ever Spring again,
>   Spring again,
> I shall go where went I when
> Down the moor-cock splashed, and hen,
> Seeing me not, amid their flounder,
> Standing with my arm around her;
> If it's ever spring again,
>   Spring again,
> I shall go where went I then.
>
> If it's ever summer-time,
>   Summer-time,
> With the hay crop at the prime,
> And the cuckoos — two — in rhyme,
> As they used to be, or seemed to,
> We shall do as long we've dreamed to,
> If it's ever summer-time,
>   Summer-time,
> With the hay, and bees achime.

Assuming that, as with so many of Hardy's other poems, this poem is about Emma, it contains the only mention by him of any physical contact with her.

In his poem *On a Discovered Curl of Hair* (published in 1922), Hardy reflected dismally on the fact that the only physical remains of Emma that he now possessed was a curl of her hair which she had given him. The poem was composed in February 1913, which was the third month after her death:

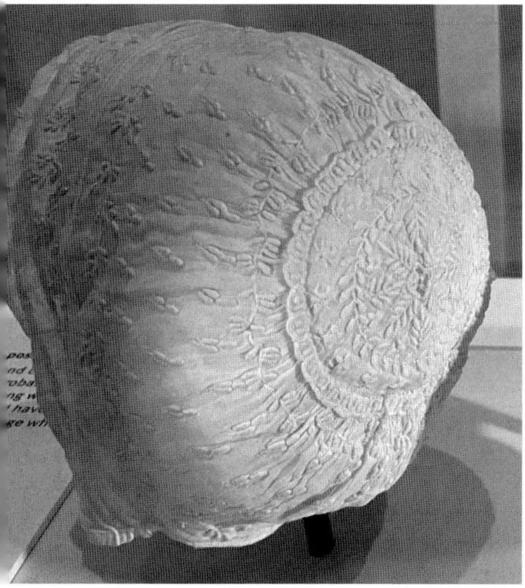

Above left: Thomas Hardy's christening bonnet, 1840. (Dorset Museum)

Above right: Thomas Hardy's spinning top, circa 1840. (Dorset Museum)

The earliest known photograph of Thomas Hardy, taken in 1856 when he was aged 16, by pioneering Dorchester photographer John Pouncey. (Dorset Museum)

His pet rabbit 'Juno I', watercolour on paper, painted by Hardy in 1856 when he was age 16. (Dorset Museum)

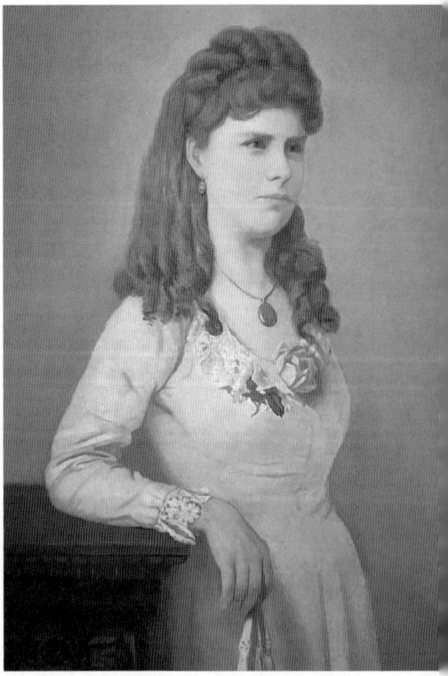

Above left: Portrait of Thomas Hardy senior (1811-1892) by his daughter Mary Hardy, oil on canvas, circa 1870. (Dorset Museum)

Above right: Emma Lavinia Gifford in 1870, aged 30, portrait by an unknown artist, donated to the Dorset Museum by Emma's nephew Gordon Gifford in 1949. (Dorset Museum)

A sketch of Emma entitled 'Searching for the Glass', made by Hardy on one of his occasional visits to Cornwall after they had first met, pencil on paper, 1870. (Dorset Museum)

Bench ends, church of St Julitta, St Juliot, Cornwall, 1870, by Thomas Hardy, pen and ink on paper. (Dorset Museum)

Sketch of the steamer *Heather Bell* by Emma: 'Going from Swanage to Ryde & all round the Isle of Wight', 1876. (Dorset Museum)

Above left: North door, church of St Julitta, St Juliot, Cornwall, 1870, by Thomas Hardy, pen and ink on paper. (Dorset Museum)

Above right: Portrait of Jemima Hardy (1813-1904) by her daughter Mary, oil on canvas, circa 1880. (Dorset Museum)

Painting by Mary Hardy of Thomas Hardy's birthplace at Higher Bockhampton, Dorset, including his mother Jemima and sister Kate, oil on canvas. (Dorset Museum)

Above: Max Gate: Emma's attic room. (The National Trust)

Right: Hardy's walking stick in wood by unknown maker, carving of a dog on its handle, with Hardy's initials carved on the back. (Dorset Museum)

Below: Pen case, late 19th century by an unknown artist, which Hardy kept on his desk in his study at Max Gate. Of black lacquered and painted wood, it is decorated with a dragonfly, a fish, and a squirrel, reflecting his love of nature. (Dorset Museum)

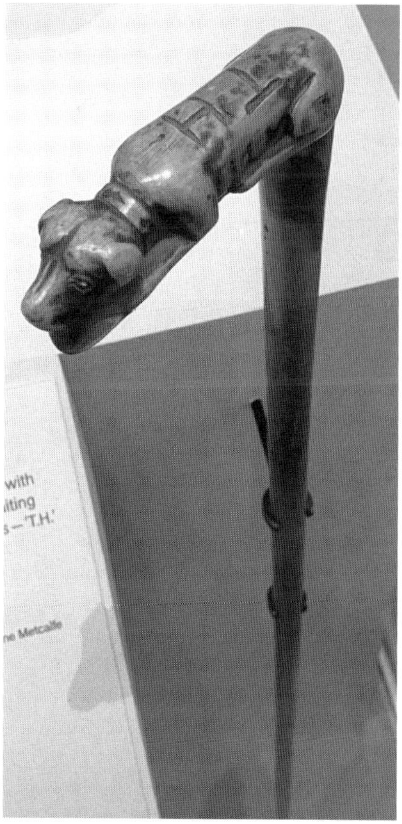

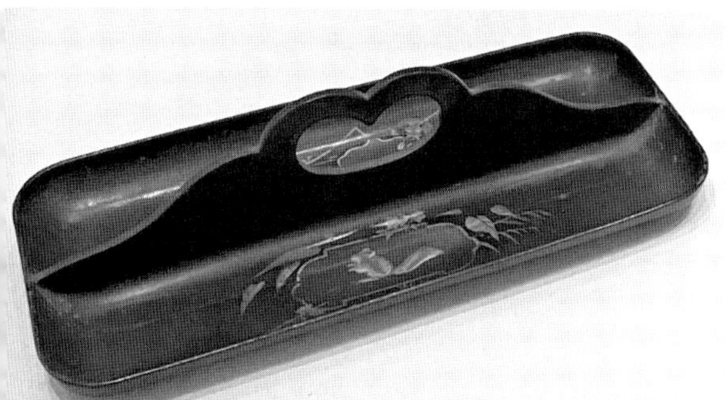

Hardy with his bicycle in the grounds of Max Gate in 1901, unknown photographer. (Dorset Museum)

Thomas Hardy's writing pens (1890-1895) with which he wrote *Tess of the D'Urbervilles* and *Jude the Obscure*. The pens were engraved 'Tess' and 'Jude' respectively. (Dorset Museum)

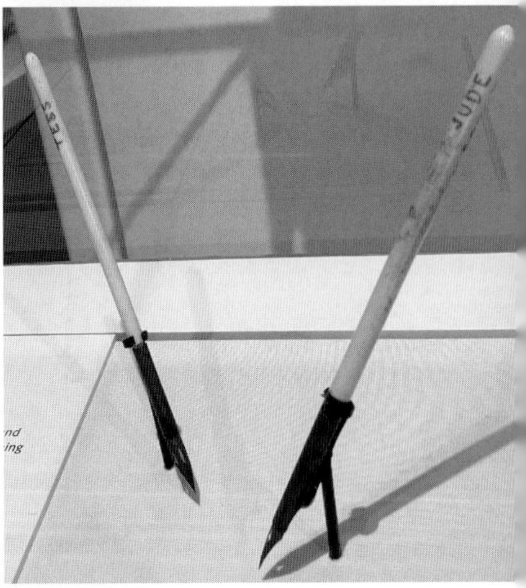

Thomas Hardy and Florence at Aldeburgh, August 1909. (Dorset Museum)

Above left: The Order of Merit, awarded to Hardy in 1910. (Dorset Museum)

Above right: Gilt casket, which contained the Freedom Scroll presented to Hardy when he was made an Honorary Freeman of the Borough of Dorchester in 1910. (Dorset Museum)

Above left: Emma Hardy with her cat 'Snowdove', circa 1910, by an unknown photographer. (Dorset Museum)

Above right: Florence Hardy with 'Wessex', circa 1910, photographed by Rodway Gardner. (Dorset Museum)

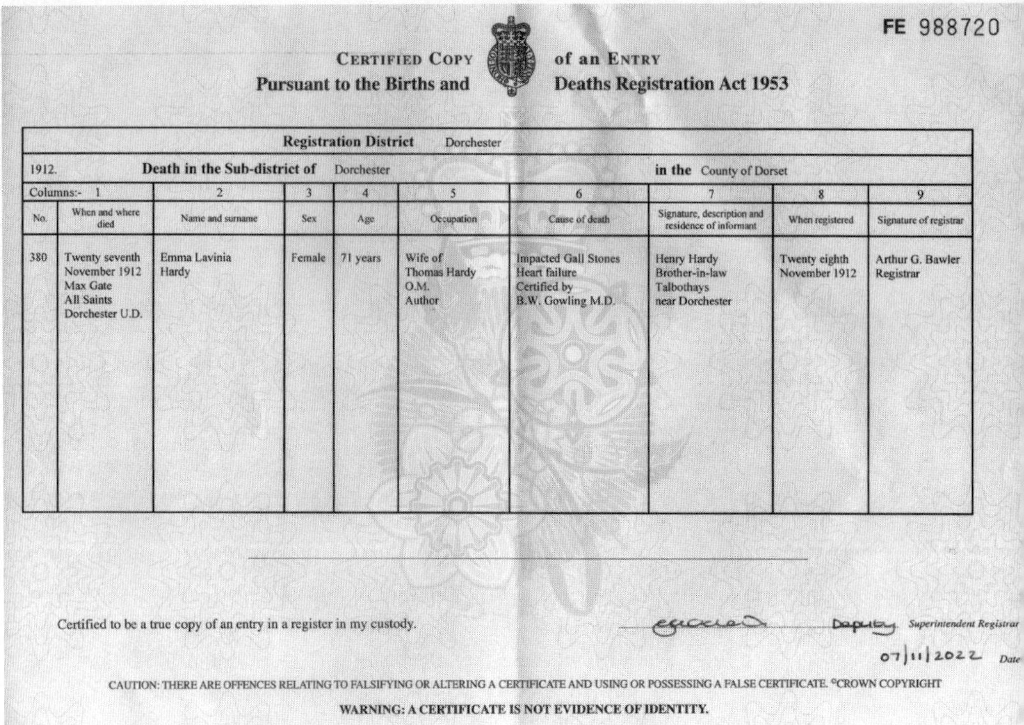

FE 988720

CERTIFIED COPY of an ENTRY
Pursuant to the Births and Deaths Registration Act 1953

Registration District Dorchester									
1912. Death in the Sub-district of Dorchester						in the County of Dorset			
Columns:- 1		2	3	4	5	6	7	8	9
No.	When and where died	Name and surname	Sex	Age	Occupation	Cause of death	Signature, description and residence of informant	When registered	Signature of registrar
380	Twenty seventh November 1912 Max Gate All Saints Dorchester U.D.	Emma Lavinia Hardy	Female	71 years	Wife of Thomas Hardy O.M. Author	Impacted Gall Stones Heart failure Certified by B.W. Gowling M.D.	Henry Hardy Brother-in-law Talbothays near Dorchester	Twenty eighth November 1912	Arthur G. Bawler Registrar

Certified to be a true copy of an entry in a register in my custody.

Deputy Superintendent Registrar

07/11/2022 Date

CAUTION: THERE ARE OFFENCES RELATING TO FALSIFYING OR ALTERING A CERTIFICATE AND USING OR POSSESSING A FALSE CERTIFICATE. ©CROWN COPYRIGHT

WARNING: A CERTIFICATE IS NOT EVIDENCE OF IDENTITY.

Emma Hardy's death certificate.

Memorial tablet erected in the church of St Julitta, St Juliot, Cornwall to Emma by Hardy after his wife's death on 27 November 1912. (Dorset Museum)

Above left: Thomas and Florence Hardy with 'Wessex' at Max Gate in 1914. Photographed by E. O. Hoppé. (Dorset Museum)

Above right: Ink sketch by Thomas Hardy of Beeny Cliff, North Cornwall, circa 1917. (Dorset Museum)

Right: The 'Poets' Tribute' book, compiled and presented to Hardy in 1919 on his 79th birthday by Siegfried Sassoon. (Dorset Museum)

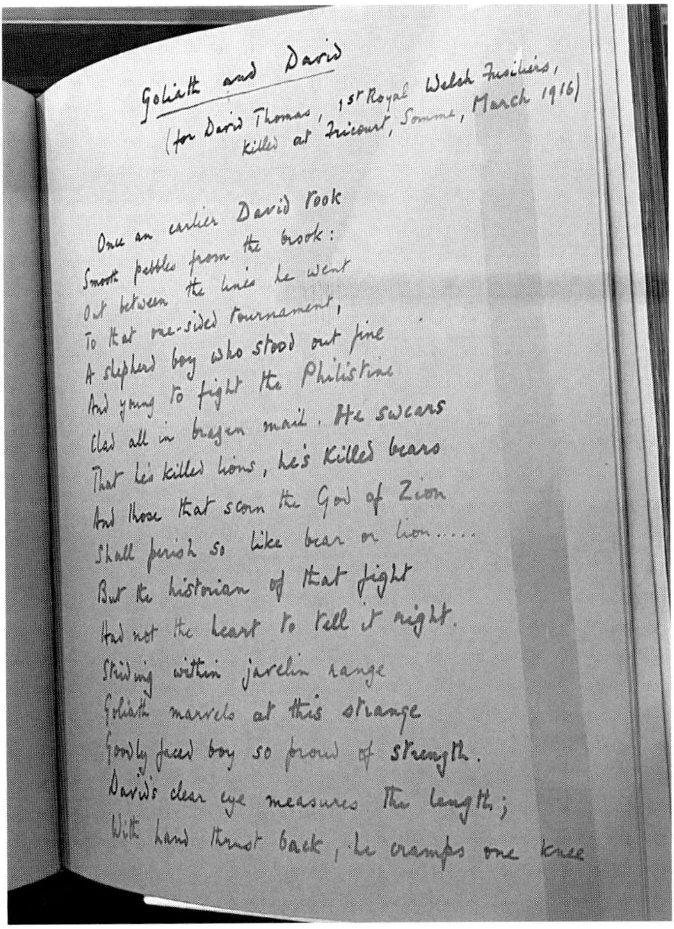

Thomas and Florence Hardy with the Prince of Wales at Max Gate in 1923. (Dorset Museum)

Above left: Albert Einstein, circa 1923. Photo: Nobel foundation, A. B. Lagrelius & Westphal. (*Wikimedia Commons*)

Above right: Hardy's copy of Albert Einstein's *Relativity*. (Dorset Museum)

Above left: Hardy's design for the tombstone of his beloved dog 'Wessex', which he carved himself, pencil on paper, circa 1926. (Dorset Museum)

Above right: Hardy with his cat 'Pandora' in 1927 in the drawing room at Max Gate. Photographed by Mrs Rees. This was the last photograph taken of Hardy. (Dorset Museum)

Max Gate: The Pet Cemetery, 'Wessex's grave in foreground. (The National Trust)

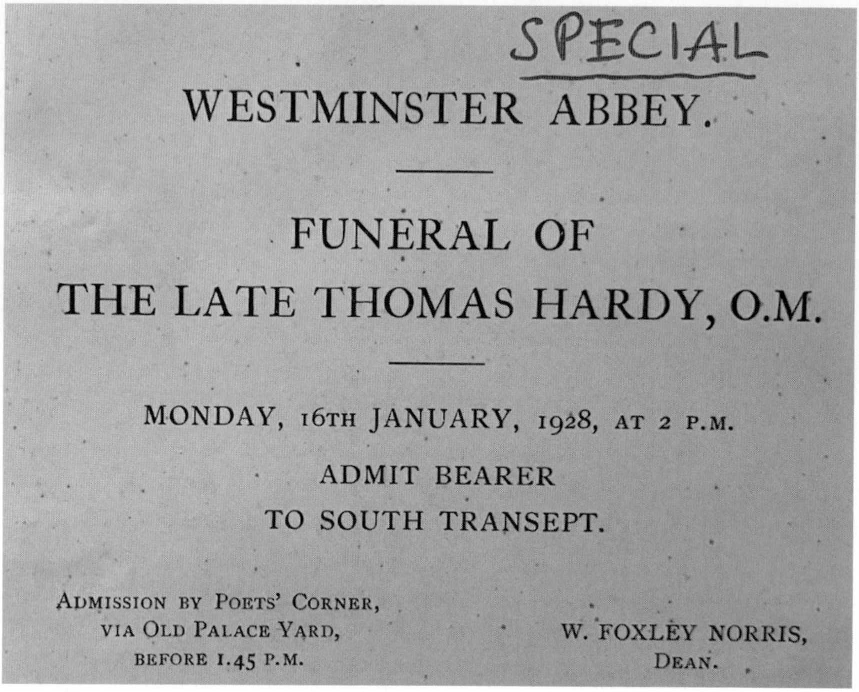

SPECIAL

WESTMINSTER ABBEY.

FUNERAL OF
THE LATE THOMAS HARDY, O.M.

MONDAY, 16TH JANUARY, 1928, AT 2 P.M.

ADMIT BEARER
TO SOUTH TRANSEPT.

ADMISSION BY POETS' CORNER,
VIA OLD PALACE YARD,
BEFORE 1.45 P.M.

W. FOXLEY NORRIS,
DEAN.

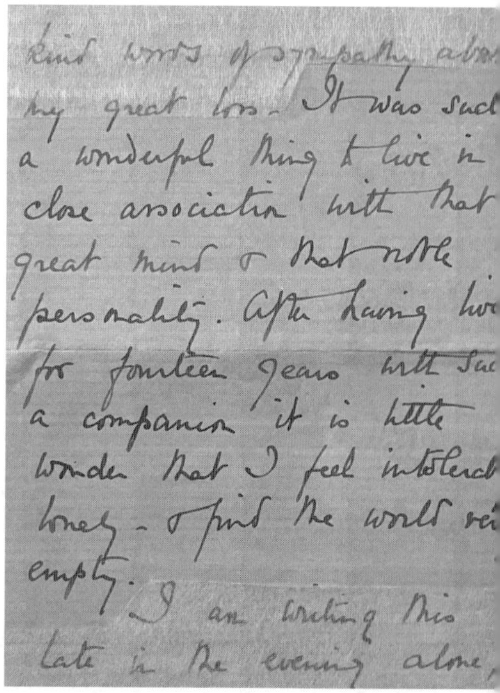

kind words of sympathy abo
my great loss. It was such
a wonderful thing to live in
close association with that
great mind & that noble
personality. After having liv
for fourteen years with suc
a companion it is little
wonder that I feel intolerab
lonely & find the world ver
empty.
I am writing this
late in the evening alone,

Above left: Church of St Michael, Stinsford: tombs of the Hardy family, including Hardy's siblings, Mary, Henry, and Katharine; Hardy's first wife Emma; Hardy's second wife Florence; Hardy's father Thomas; Hardy's mother Jemima. Hardy's heart is buried in the tomb containing Emma and Florence.

Above right: Extract of a letter from Florence Hardy to Harold Barlow, 20 February 1932. (Dorset History Centre)

Right: The author and his beloved late wife (Alison) Rachel Norman (née Jordan) at Hardy's birthplace, Higher Bockhampton, near Dorchester, Dorset.

Below: Max Gate. (The National Trust)

Max Gate, from the kitchen garden. (The National Trust)

The author at Max Gate.

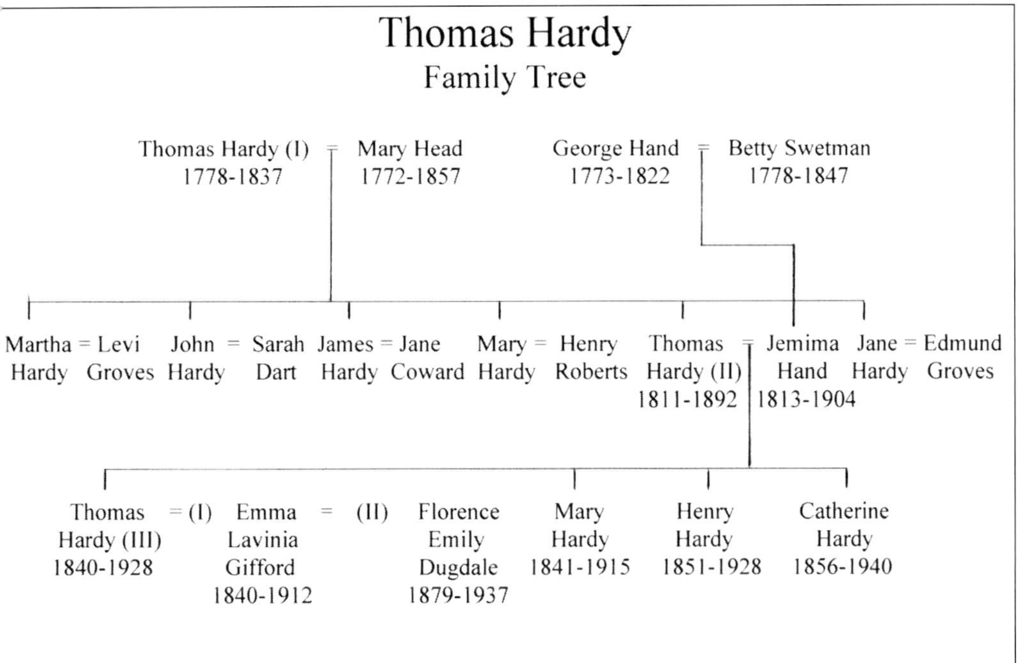

'Catherine' is the spelling on her birth certificate, though her name is often spelt 'Katharine'.

Hardy Family Tree.

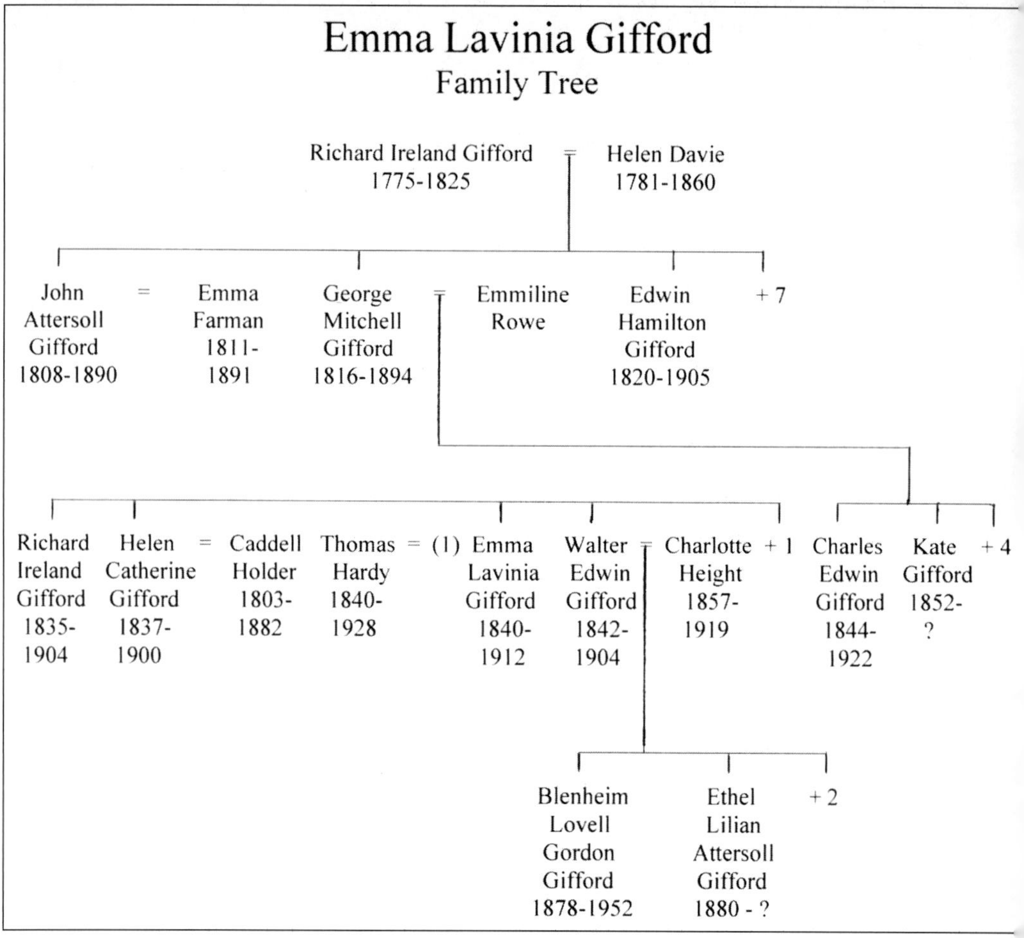

Emma's Family Tree.

When your soft welcomings were said,
This curl was waving on your head,
And when we walked where breakers dinned
It sported in the sun and wind,
And when I had won your words of grace
It brushed and clung about my face.
Then, to abate the misery
Of absentness, you gave it me.

Where are its fellows now? Ah, they
For brightest brown have donned a gray,
And gone into a caverned ark,
Ever unopened, always dark!

Yet this one curl, untouched of time,
Beams with live brown as in its prime,
So that it seems I even could now
Restore it to the living brow
By bearing down the western road
Till I had reached your old abode.

Absentness: presumably when Hardy had to return home to Dorset after his visits to Emma in Cornwall.

In other words, Hardy imagined returning to Emma's 'old abode' – St Julitta's Rectory – and restoring the curl to its rightful owner.

In his poem *Beeny Cliff* (published in 1914), the scene of Hardy's courtship of Emma, he recognized that now she was deceased, she was beyond knowing or caring for that place anymore, let alone remembering it or revisiting it with him:

I
O the opal and the sapphire of that wandering western sea,
And the woman riding high above with bright hair flapping free -
The woman whom I loved so, and who loyally loved me.

IV
– Still in all its chasmal beauty bulks old Beeny to the sky,
And shall she and I not go there once again now March is nigh,
And the sweet things said in that March say anew there by and by?

V
What if still in chasmal beauty looms that wild weird western shore,
The woman now is – elsewhere - whom the ambling pony bore,
And nor knows nor cares for Beeny, and will laugh there nevermore.

Here is Hardy once again affirming, not only that he had once loved Emma, but that she had loved him and been loyal to him.

8. How Hardy Longed to be at Peace

In his poem *A Wish for Unconsciousness* (published in 1928), Hardy imagined himself as being deceased, with only a memorial tablet, or his grave, or his portrait remaining, in which case he would feel pain no more.

If I could but abide
As a tablet on a wall,
Or a hillock daisy-pied,
Or a picture in a hall,
And as nothing else at all,
I should feel no doleful achings,
I should hear no judgment-call,
Have no evil dreams or wakings,
No uncouth or grisly care;
In a word, no cross to bear.

Chapter 10

Hardy's Feelings of Guilt over his Treatment of Emma

Hardy's poem *The Peace-Offering* (published in 1917, the fifth year after Emma's death), contained only two verses but they are revealing:

> It was but a little thing,
> Yet I knew it meant to me
> Ease from what had given a sting
> To the very birdsinging
> Latterly.
>
> But I would not welcome it;
> And for all I then declined
> O the regrettings infinite
> When the night-processions flit
> Through the mind!

Writer and Hardy scholar F. B. Pinion explained that the poem came to be written as a result of Hardy's:

> 'rejection at a small attempt [by Emma] at reconciliation', after she 'had wounded his feelings ….' The fact that he had rejected this 'peace offering' by Emma 'now became a continual reproach to him'.[1]

A few days before Emma's death, she and Hardy were involved in a violent quarrel. Said Flower:

> 'It so happened that Emma Hardy came into this room [Hardy's study] on one occasion when he had just finished his midday meal. She stood there surveying the room — this room that was now a [presumably protective] "shell" about her husband. She saw the

> table littered with the remains of food, and high words ensued. In that room — in a few moments of Time — they broke apart after years of passive defence.'
>
> 'A few days later Emma Hardy was taken ill. Seriously ill. Very soon she was dead, and Hardy took full blame upon himself. If he had only kept silent a little longer with that passive acceptance of discord which had been his through the later years! The real cause of death was ulcer of the stomach, but Hardy believed that this, their first and last outburst of violent quarrel, had hastened her illness. He never departed from that belief. It remained with him as a means of self-castigation till his last years ....'[2]

In this, Flower was incorrect. The post-mortem examination, as already mentioned, stated the cause of death to be 'Impacted Gall Stones' and 'Heart Failure'. It is unlikely, therefore, that an argument with Hardy could have directly precipitated Emma's death.

A gallstone is a small, hard, crystalline mass formed abnormally in the gall bladder or bile ducts from bile pigments, cholesterol, and calcium salts.[3]

Gall bladder: the small sac-shaped organ beneath the liver, in which bile is stored after secretion by the liver and before release into the intestine.[4]

An impacted gall stone is one which blocks the cystic duct (leading from gall bladder to common bile duct), or the common bile duct (the conduit for bile from the liver and gall bladder to the intestine); or the pancreatic duct (the conduit for pancreatic juices to the common bile duct). Blockage of the bile duct leads to inflammation of the gall bladder (cholecystitis) and infection; blockage of the pancreas leads to inflammation of the pancreas (pancreatitis) and infection. The pain and shock caused by either condition, pancreatitis in particular, may precipitate heart failure, particularly in an elderly person like Emma, who three days before her death had reached the age of 72.

To Florence Henniker on 17 December 1912 Hardy wrote of Emma's final illness:

> 'I have reproached myself for not having guessed there might be some internal mischief at work, instead of blindly supposing her robust & sound & likely to live to quite old age.'[5]

On 20 April 1913, in a letter to Clodd, Florence described how Hardy's doctor (Edward W. Mann) had declared that: 'the state of things here, before Mrs Hardy's death - was quite alarming, so far as T. H. [Thomas Hardy] was concerned. He [Mann] said that the lack of attention & general discomfort must have had a serious effect, sooner or later. He told this to the [i.e. Hardy's] sisters & brother'.[6] The implication of this is that Hardy was indeed neglectful of his wife Emma, at any rate towards the end of her life. So yes, perhaps Hardy *did* have something to feel guilty about!

By contrast, to museum curator and collector Sydney Cockerell on 26 April 1916, Hardy wrote:

> 'I have a Bath chair [a kind of wheelchair for invalids, typically with a hood[7]] of the very best make & appearance, which I bought for my late wife, & which she used a little though not much. If you will accept this chair as a gift from me for the use of Mrs Cockrell I shall be delighted. The thought of selling it has always gone rather against my feeling, so my compunctions would be removed by your having it.'[8]

Cockerell's wife Florence (née Kingsford) had been diagnosed with multiple sclerosis in that same year.

Surely, to put matters in perspective, the provision of a wheelchair for Emma by Hardy was an instance of a caring gesture on his part.

As if to compound Hardy's guilt feelings, he was under the impression that Emma held him responsible for her suffering, as his poem *I Thought, my Heart* (published in 1917) indicates. In the poem, Hardy described his late wife Emma as a traumatized person who believed that he was totally responsible for the pain and misery that she had endured during their marriage:

> I thought, my Heart, that you had healed
> Of those sore smartings of the past,
> And that the summers had oversealed
> All mark of them at last.
> But closely scanning in the night
> I saw them standing crimson-bright
> Just as she made them:
> Nothing could fade them;
> Yea, I can swear
> That there they were -
> They still were there!
>
> Then the Vision of her who cut them came,
> And looking over my shoulder said,
> "I am sure you deal me all the blame
> For those sharp smarts and red;
> But meet me, dearest, to-morrow night,

In the churchyard at the moon's half-height,
And so strange a kiss
Shall be mine, I wis,
That you'll cease to know
If the wounds you show
Be there or no!"

I wis: I am certain, sure.

Chapter 11

Did Hardy and Emma Have Anything in Common at all?

Emma and Hardy had in common that they both enjoyed watercolour painting and sketching, and many of their works survive.

A topic on which Hardy and Emma did see eye to eye was women's suffrage (the right to vote in political elections[1] and the victimization of women in general, which was abhorrent to both of them. Emma was actively involved in suffrage, aimed at giving women the right to vote in political elections. In this, she was fully supported by Hardy).

Hardy was also outraged by the fact that a woman who bore a child out of wedlock was automatically ostracized by the church. Not only that, in his novel *Far from the Madding Crowd* (published in 1874), he indicated that in his opinion, women in his day had a raw deal. For example, the heroine Bathsheba Everdene affirmed that:

> 'It is difficult for a woman to define her feelings in language which is chiefly made by men to express theirs.'[2]

Animal welfare was another crusade for Hardy and Emma. To Florence Henniker on 17 December 1912 Hardy wrote of Emma:

> 'I think I have told you before that her *courage* in the cause of animals was truly admirable, surpassing that of any other woman I have ever known.'[3]

Hardy was deeply concerned not only for his fellow man and woman, but also for all creatures. In 1904, he wrote, 'What are my books but one plea against man's inhumanity to man - to woman - and to the lower animals?'[4]

When Hardy and Emma's pets died they were buried in the garden of Max Gate, often with a headstone, a tradition that was maintained even after Emma's death. For example, said Florence, their fox terrier 'Wessex', who died on 27 December 1926, 'lies in a small, turfed grave in the shrubbery on the west side of Max Gate'. 'Wessex' originally belonged to Florence, but Hardy soon became inordinately fond of him, hence his nickname!

Wessex: the kingdom of the West Saxons, established in Hampshire in the early sixth century and gradually extended by conquest to include much of southern England. The name was revived in the nineteenth century by Thomas Hardy to designate the south-western counties of England (especially Dorset) in which his novels are set.[5]

'Wessex's headstone reads as follows:

THE
FAMOUS DOG

WESSEX

AUG. 1913-27 DEC. 1926
FAITHFUL, UNFLINCHING

> 'Wessex' was, arguably, the most badly behaved dog in England, undoubtedly because Hardy indulged him to the nth degree. However, said Florence, 'There were those among Hardy's friends who thought that his life was definitely saddened by the loss of 'Wessex''. Also, in the pet cemetery, 'were buried several pet cats and one other dog'.[6]

As all those who keep dogs know, they are a constant in one's life and can be relied upon to give unconditional love and loyalty.

In his poem *Dead 'Wessex' the Dog to the Household* (published in 1928), Hardy wondered if his beloved late canine companion (and indeed other former pets) ever thought of him, even though 'Wessex' was deceased:

I
Do you think of me at all,
    Wistful ones?
Do you think of me at all
    As if nigh?
Do you think of me at all
At the creep of evenfall,
Or when the sky-birds call
    As they fly?

II
Do you look for me at times,
    Wistful ones?
Do you look for me at times
    Strained and still?
Do you look for me at times,
When the hour for walking chimes,
On that grassy path that climbs
    Up the hill?

A bone of contention between Hardy and Emma was the subject of religion. Hardy was a religious sceptic and unlike Emma, who was a religious zealot, he did not attend church. However, as Evelyn Hardy pointed out:

> 'Emma Hardy still had hopes of leading her husband back to a more conventional faith'. This 'is evidenced by her gift to him of the Holy Bible inscribed "T. Hardy from E. L. H., June 2, 1899, Wynstay Gardens, Kensington".'[7]

Chapter 12

Emma's Mental State

1. Hardy and Others were Aware that Emma was Mentally Unstable

Hardy himself was only too well aware that Emma's mind was somewhat disordered. On 16 February 1914, he wrote to the Reverend J. H. Dickinson (Rector of St Juliot from 1906-1925) to say:

> 'If ever ghosts revisit old scenes I am sure mine will haunt S. Juliot by reason of the experiences I was there blest with before my first marriage, & long before the sadness came that was a result of the slight mental aberration which occasionally afflicted my wife's latter years.'[1]

To poet and novelist Florence Henniker on 6 March 1914, Hardy wrote regarding his marriage to Florence on 10 February of the previous month:

> 'I am rather surprised that *you* were surprised at the step we have taken - such a course seeming an obvious one to me, being as I was so lonely & helpless. I think I told you in my last letter that I am very glad she [Florence] knew Emma well & was liked by her even during her latter years, when her [Emma's] mind was a little unhinged at times, & she showed unreasonable dislikes.'

Nevertheless, Hardy continued to cherish the memory of Emma as she had been in her prime:

> 'I wonder if it will surprise you when I say that according to my own experience of second marriage *does not*, or need not, obliterate an old affection, though it is generally assumed that the first wife is entirely forgotten in such cases.'[2]

On 23 November 1914 Hardy wrote to Emma's cousin Kate Gifford to say:

> 'I am sending you my new volume of poems - not because I think you will care for a large number of them, but because it contains some that relate to Emma. From what I have found among her memoranda I see that she had a great affection for you & your sister. In later years an unfortunate mental aberration for which she was not responsible altered her much & made her cold in her correspondence with friends & relatives, but this was contrary to her real nature, & I myself quite disregard it in thinking of her. She was, as you know, most childlike and trusting formerly. You may be able to perceive some of her characteristics in the poems about her.'[3]

Hardy, however, was not the only person to notice that Emma could act strangely and inappropriately, far from it. Christine Wood Homer of Athelhampton Hall was a friend of the Hardys. She described how, if a visitor arrived at Max Gate and Emma suspected that the person had 'no interest in or friendship for her but had come only to see Mr Hardy and worship at his shrine', she would not inform her husband of the presence of that visitor, who would go away 'without seeing his hero'.

Emma 'would have liked to have received the admiration of the world for talents she believed she possessed', but according to Christine, the poems that she wrote were 'indifferent', and as for her talents, they were 'not discernible to anybody else'. Christine stated that Emma 'had the fixed idea that she was the superior of her husband in birth, education, talents, and manners. She could not, and never did, recognize his greatness'. In other words, Christine believed that Emma suffered from delusions in respect of her abilities.

Delusion: an idiosyncratic belief or impression maintained despite being contradicted by reality or rational argument, typically as a symptom of mental disorder.[4]

In summary, Christine described Emma as 'a peculiar woman, and in many ways like a little child'; but whereas at first 'she had only been childish, with advancing age [she] became very queer and talked curiously'. Finally, said Christine, it had been 'a burdensome grief' to Hardy that Emma 'had not cared for any of his family'.[5]

Lorna Heenan was the daughter of Dr Frederick B. Fisher, who (until he retired in 1910) was Hardy's medical adviser. Lorna stated that Emma's:

> 'mental condition progressively deteriorated, with a consequential increased strain on her husband. [Also, her] "heretical" outbursts in the local papers caused her husband great embarrassment'.[6]
>
> As for Dr Fisher himself, he was of the opinion that Emma was 'the cause of much of the great man's pessimism and depression'.[7]

Evelyn Evans was the daughter of Alfred H. Evans: by day a chemist, but by night a producer of Hardy's plays for the Dorchester Debating, Literary, and Dramatic Society. Evelyn, who, from an early age had been taught to 'reverence' Hardy, described the 'mauve, satin ribbons' that used to wave from Emma Hardy's bonnet as she bicycled around the town. 'She was considered very odd by the townspeople [of Dorchester]', said Evelyn, who would 'touch their foreheads significantly as she went by, free-wheeling … with her feet off the pedals'.[8] According to Evelyn, during Emma's later years:

> 'her delusions of grandeur grew more marked. Never forgetting [that] she was an archdeacon's niece [a reference to Emma's uncle, the Reverend Edwin Hamilton Gifford, Archdeacon of London who had conducted her marriage ceremony], who had married beneath her, she was heard to say in front of guests, "Try to remember, Thomas Hardy, that you married a lady". She persuaded embarrassed editors to publish her worthless poems, and intimated that she was the guiding spirit of all Hardy's work.'[9]

The writers A. C. Benson and Edmund Gosse visited Max Gate together in September 1912. Benson, who had not met Emma before, described her as:

> 'A small, pretty, rather mincing elderly lady with hair curiously puffed & padded [and] rather fantastically dressed. It was hard to talk to Mrs H. who rambled along in a very inconsequential way, with a bird-like sort of wit, looking sideways & treating my remarks as amiable interruptions.'

Mince: to walk with short, quick steps in an affectedly dainty manner.[10]

As Emma showed him, 'in a curious, peering way', the drawing room at Max Gate, said Benson, she talked 'in a hurried voice, as if she was thinking aloud and not regarding me at all'. In the garden, Emma became obsessed with pinching the pods of the plant *noli-me-tangere* (yellow balsam) in order to make them eject their seeds. 'Mrs Hardy got entirely absorbed in this & went on doing it with little jumps and elfin shrieks of pleasure.'

The visit to Max Gate, said Benson, left him with:

> 'a melancholy impression. It gave me a sense of something intolerable the thought of his [Hardy] having to live day & night with the absurd, inconsequent, huffy, rambling old lady. They don't get on together at all. The marriage was thought a misalliance for her, when he was poor & undistinguished, and she continues to resent it.'

As for Hardy, said Benson: 'He is not agreeable to her either, but his patience must be incredibly tried. She is so queer, & yet has to be treated as rational while she is full, I imagine, of suspicions & jealousies & affronts which must be half insane'.[11]

On 17 December 1912, in a letter to Florence Henniker, Hardy wrote in regard to himself and Emma of 'the differences between us, which it would be an affectation to deny', and of 'certain painful delusions [which] she suffered from at times'.[12]

In July 1913 Edward Clodd visited Max Gate where he was introduced to Hardy's brother Henry, whom he described as 'a well-set, sensible man', and his two sisters, whom he described as 'ladylike, refined' and 'well-informed'. However, Clodd remonstrated with Hardy for allowing his 'half-mad wife' to deny his family – 'these well-bred folk as well as his mother [Jemima]' - access to Max Gate.[13]

On 25 November 1914 Emma's cousin, Kate Gifford, wrote to Hardy thus:

> 'Emma and I met at my brother's at Blackheath not long before her death & I was so glad to see her again. It must have been very sad for you that her mind became so unbalanced latterly'.[14]

Is it possible that all the aforementioned people, who had met Emma at first hand, were wrong in their assessment of her? No, of course not! The conclusion is, therefore, that Emma had developed a significant mental health problem, which, as even Kate Gifford, a member of her own family acknowledged, became progressively worse as the years wore on.[15]

In 1920 publisher Vere H. Collins, during a series of discussions with Hardy at Max Gate, made an important breakthrough, when he questioned the latter about his poem *The Interloper* (published in 1917), which he could not make sense of. It reads as follows:

> There are three folk driving in a quaint old chaise,
> And the cliff-side track looks green and fair;
> I view them talking in quiet glee

As they drop down towards the puffins' lair
    By the roughest of ways;
But another with the three rides on, I see,
    Whom I like not to be there!

No: it's not anybody you think of. Next
A dwelling appears by a slow sweet stream
Where two sit happily and half in the dark:
They read, helped out by a frail-wick'd gleam,
    Some rhythmic text;
But one sits with them whom they don't mark,
    One I'm wishing could not be there.

No: not whom you knew and name. And now
I discern gay diners in a mansion-place,
And the guests dropping wit—pert, prim, or choice,
And the hostess's tender and laughing face,
    And the host's bland brow;
But I cannot help hearing a hollow voice,
    And I'd fain not hear it there.

No: it's not from the stranger you once met. Ah,
Yet a goodlier scene than that succeeds;
People on a lawn—quite a crowd of them. Yes,
And they chatter and ramble as fancy leads;
    And they say, 'Hurrah!'
To a blithe speech made; save one, mirthless,
    Who ought not to be there.

Nay: it's not the pale Form your imagings raise,
That waits on us all at a destined time,
It is not the Fourth Figure the Furnace showed;
O that it were such a shape sublime
    In these latter days!
It is that under which best lives corrode;
    Would, would it could not be there!

How may the above poem be explained? In her book *Some Recollections*, Emma described how, in the intervals between Hardy's visits to St Juliot over 4½ years, from the date when he first met her on 7 March 1870 to the date of their marriage on 17 September 1874, she would drive her brother-in-law the Reverend Cadell Holder, and her sister Helen, Holder's wife, in the basket-carriage (a carriage with a body of wickerwork, drawn by a horse or pony).[16] These are therefore the 'three folk referred to in Verse I. But who is the unknown, nameless and humourless fourth person, who only Hardy could see and hear and who he wished was not present? And was this person real or imagined?

In Verse V, the 'pale Form' may refer to Saint Peter, who is said to guard the gates of heaven. 'The Fourth Figure the Furnace showed' derives from the Book of Daniel in the *Holy Bible*'s Old Testament. Nebuchadnezzar II, King of Babylon was told that three men, Shadrach, Meshach and Abednego, 'have not regarded thee: they serve not thy gods, nor worship the golden image which thou hast set up'. Whereupon the King ordered that they be 'cast … into the burning fiery furnace'. However, not only did the three men emerge unscathed, but a fourth man appeared, whose form was 'like the Son of God'.[17]

Collins's interrogation of Hardy led to some extraordinary revelations. When Collins asked Hardy to explain the penultimate line of the poem, 'that under which best lives corrode', Hardy replied: 'Madness'. Whereupon Collins asked, 'In each case?' [i.e. in each of the 'lives'], to which Hardy retorted, 'Yes. I knew the family'.[18]

When Collins suggested that Hardy give *The Interloper* a subtitle, in order to make its meaning clearer, Hardy, in the 1923 edition of *Moments of Vision*, did just that, and the subtitle he chose was both startling and shocking: 'And I saw the figure and visage of Madness seeking for a home'. Said Collins:

> 'When Hardy uttered that word ['madness'] … there burst on me a revelation. This was the clue. *The Blow*, *The Blot*, *The Wound*; the spectre haunting that beautiful girl while she sang and played; the shadow darkening and chilling that passionate union; the lovers struck by an unexpected, unprovoked, undeserved foe; now at last I grasped what … had put an end to happiness in Hardy's marriage and life – that had tended to concentrate his attention on the tragedies and ironies in love – that had accentuated the "grim message" from his reading of life.'

The insightful Collins had realized that '*The Blow*', '*The Blot*', and '*The Wound*' were expressions to be found in other poems of Hardy's.[19] For example:

The Blow

In his poem *The Blow* (published in 1917), Hardy demanded to know who had seen fit:

> To have hurled that stone
> Into the sunshine of our days!

In other words, to have blighted the lives of himself and Emma. And he concluded that it was the 'Immanent Doer' – the unseen and uncaring, if not callous and malevolent force, otherwise known by Hardy as 'The Will', that was responsible:

Time's finger should have stretched to show
No aimful author's was the blow
That swept us prone,
But the Immanent Doer's That doth not know,

Which in some age unguessed of us
May lift Its blinding incubus,
And see, and own:
'It grieves me I did thus and thus!'

In other words, the 'Immanent Doer' would one day regret his action.

'The Blot'

In his poem *Beyond the Last Lamp* (published in 1914) and subtitled 'Near Tooting Common', two lovers – Hardy and Emma, of course – had undergone thirty years of 'blur' and 'blot':

I
While rain, with eve in partnership,
Descended darkly, drip, drip, drip,
Beyond the last lone lamp I passed
Walking slowly, whispering sadly,
Two linked loiterers, wan, downcast:
Some heavy thought constrained each face,
And blinded them to time and place.

II
The pair seemed lovers, yet absorbed
In mental scenes no longer orbed
By love's young rays. Each countenance
As it slowly, as it sadly
Caught the lamplight's yellow glance
Held in suspense a misery
At things which had been or might be.

III
When I retrod that watery way
Some hours beyond the droop of day,

Still I found pacing there the twain
Just as slowly, just as sadly,
Heedless of the night and rain.
One could but wonder who they were
And what wild woe detained them there.

IV
Though thirty years of blur and blot
Have slid since I beheld that spot,
And saw in curious converse there
Moving slowly, moving sadly
That mysterious tragic pair,
Its olden look may linger on -
All but the couple; they have gone.

V
Whither? Who knows, indeed ... And yet
To me, when nights are weird and wet,
Without those comrades there at tryst
Creeping slowly, creeping sadly,
That lone lane does not exist.
There they seem brooding on their pain,
And will, while such a lane remain.

The Hardys had, in fact, lived at Tooting, London from 1878 to 1881.

The Wound
In his poem *The Wound* (published in 1917), Hardy made reference not to a physical wound, but to an inner hurt which he had chosen to keep to himself:

I climbed to the crest,
And, fog-festooned,
The sun lay west
Like a crimson wound:

Like that wound of mine
Of which none knew,
For I'd given no sign
That it pierced me through.

Again, Collins believed that Hardy had his marriage to Emma in mind when he penned these lines.

And, of course, there are a myriad of other mournful and regretful poems by Hardy on the same theme. 'How gently and with what compassionate care would Hardy have treated his wife had he fully realized her predicament' [i.e. the true extent of her illness], said Evelyn Hardy.

There is evidence that Hardy was fully aware that Emma had mental health problems *even before he married her*. Viz. Hardy's reference in *The Interloper* to the 'three folk driving in a quaint old chaise' (Emma and her sister and brother-in-law), and to 'the figure and visage of Madness seeking for a home' – a clear reference to Emma during the time she was driving her relatives around in the chaise – i.e. between her first meeting Hardy in March 1870 and her marriage to Hardy in September 1874. So why *did* he marry her? Presumably because, by his own admission, he was captivated by her beauty.

Modern science has shed light on how hormones are involved in reinforcing the sensations and bonding that occurs in loving partnerships. When two people fall in love, so-called 'love hormones' or 'cuddle hormones' – oxytocin, dopamine, and serotonin - are produced which heighten the couple's loving feelings towards one another, create a strong bond between them, and also create a sense of mutual happiness and contentment. This was surely the case for both Hardy and Emma when they first met.

Even in the later years of their marriage, it is quite possible that the love hormones were still in play, albeit if to a lesser extent and despite the apparent absence of sexual activity. Even though Hardy and Emma were virtually estranged, he may have continued to experience a frisson – sudden strong feeling of excitement[20] - and consequent release of hormones, for instance when he caught sight of Emma in the garden, or when they appeared at one of their famous garden parties together and he was captivated by her demeanour and her feminine grace, just as in days gone by at St Juliot.

To summarize, it was Collins's opinion, and he was doubtless correct, that 'the interloper' was Emma's insanity. As for Hardy, he declared in respect of the eponymous poem, 'Insanity, that is a better word than Madness'.[21]

The day after Collins had this conversation with Hardy, he met Florence who said of Emma:

> 'She was subject at times to delusions. She would then make the wildest accusations against anyone, including her husband .... At such times life with her was almost unbearable.'[22]

In other words, Florence also concurred with Collins and Hardy, that Emma's mind was at times deranged.

2. Emma's Religious Mania

In the course of her marriage to Hardy, said Flower:

> 'Emma Hardy developed a mild form of religious mania. She became eccentric. She would leave an open copy of the *Bible* on the dressing-tables of the guests' bedrooms. The page might be thick with dust before the next visitors arrived, but the message was there to be read.'[1]

In respect of Emma's 'delusions', which Hardy mentioned in a letter to Florence Henniker,[2] Gittings stated as follows:

> '"It certainly has all the marks of mild religious mania. Such mental states often attach themselves to whatever is the latest scientific invention. In the 1920s people with a degree of religious dottiness thought they were receiving divine or demonic messages through wireless waves, just as in the nineteenth century they had similar obsessions about domestic gas."[3] Emma's imagery shows a fixation on the fairly recent phenomenon of electric light.'

In her book *Spaces*, as already mentioned, Emma described the Day of Judgement - the final judgement of humanity by God at the end of the world - thus:

> 'Peoples of the world everywhere will prostrate themselves, the electric lights of the world will shine forth again, not *lit* by mortal hands which will have failed to set them aglow .... They will gleam and burn fiercely with an awful intensity toward their final burning up of the earth.'[4]

And she described the Last Trump – the trumpet blast that, it is believed, will wake the dead on Judgement Day – in this way:

> 'The ominous rumbling of thunder sounds unaccompanied by lightning or rain will precede the gradual rising of a sound, terrible, penetrating, continuous, and arresting attention, producing fear, paralyzing effort, after awhile stopping all energy whatever and causing a general distress of nations, which calling to each other to know if this thunder is everywhere to be heard receive terrifying confirmation. And then will occur the general darkening of the sun, moon, and stars by blackest clouds, as at the Crucifixion, and the power of that awful trumpet accelerated

> till the final blast, when suddenly a spot of light will appear in the East at 4 a.m. according to western time — and dark night of eastern time or about that hour, varying at distances, the hot sunshine there gone completely, leaving, however, the weariness and dreariness of afternoon heat of hot latitudes. And while bodies will be seen rising and floating in the phosphorescent great oceans, in seas, lakes, rivers, the graveyards will be crowded with strange moving figures seen dimly in the darkness and that much watched spot of Eastern light will brighten and be enlarged ….'[5]

Aside from Emma's poor grammar and punctuation, these are clearly not the workings of a normal mind!

3. Emma's Mental State: A Likely Diagnosis

Is there a diagnosis which is appropriate for Emma's undoubted mental disorder? In the *Diagnostic and Statistical Manual of Mental Disorders* (Fifth Edition, published in 2013 by the American Psychiatric Association), psychiatrists describe a variety of 'Personality Disorders', for example, 'Narcissistic Personality Disorder', the 'essential feature' of which is:

> 'a pervasive pattern of grandiosity, need for admiration, and lack of empathy that begins by early adulthood ….'

Grandiose: extravagantly or pretentiously imposing in appearance or style.[1]

> 'Individuals with this disorder have a grandiose sense of self-importance. They routinely overestimate their abilities and inflate their accomplishments, often appearing boastful and pretentious. They may blithely assume that others attribute the same values to their efforts and may be surprised when the praise they expect and feel they deserve is not forthcoming. Often implicit in the inflated judgments of their own accomplishments is an underestimation (devaluation) of the contributions of others.'
>
> 'Individuals with narcissistic personality disorder believe that they are superior, special, or unique, and expect others to recognize them as such. They may feel that they can only be understood by and should only associate with, other people who are special or of high status ….'
>
> 'Individuals with this disorder generally require excessive admiration. [However] Their self-esteem is almost invariably

> very fragile. They may be preoccupied with how well they are doing and how favorably they are regarded by others. This often takes the form of a need for constant attention and admiration. They may expect their arrival to be greeted with great fanfare ....'
>
> 'Arrogant, haughty behaviors characterize these individuals; they often display snobbish, disdainful, or patronizing attitudes.'
>
> 'Vulnerability in self-esteem makes individuals with narcissistic personality disorder very sensitive to "injury" from criticism or defeat. Although they may not show it outwardly, criticism may haunt these individuals and may leave them feeling humiliated, degraded, hollow, and empty. They may react with disdain, rage, or defiant counterattack. Such experiences often lead to social withdrawal or an appearance of humility that may mask and protect the grandiosity. Interpersonal relations are typically impaired because of problems derived from entitlement, the need for admiration, and the relative disregard for the sensitivities of others.'[2]

From the accounts of Emma's behaviour and mannerisms as given by visitors to the Hardy household and acquaintances of the Hardys, by a member of Emma's own family, and of course by Hardy, and by his second wife Florence, it is clear that the above depiction of the typical narcissist fits Emma like the proverbial glove. Nonetheless, Alice 'Dolly' Gale, her personal maid, attested to the fact that Emma was capable of kindness, thoughtfulness, and generosity, as will be seen.

Just as Hardy became increasing disillusioned with Emma as the years went by, so she herself became disillusioned with him. This is evident in a letter that Emma wrote to literary critic Clement Shorter in about 1898, in which she said of Hardy: 'He is like no other man, nor himself as he *was*'.[3]

Chapter 13

Hardy's Mental State

Was Hardy a narcissist, and did his marriage to Emma fail because he was totally selfish and absorbed with himself? Not during those early, heady days of their courtship, certainly. And in other respects, Hardy showed a great deal of empathy: for animals, for example; for the Dorsetshire labourer, about whom he wrote a pamphlet; for the sick, viz. his visits to various hospitals including Swanage; for German prisoners of war during the First World War; and of course in his novels, where he highlighted the plight of the poor, the oppressed, and the underprivileged like no other UK author except, perhaps, Charles Dickens. But as already indicated, as the years went by Hardy became less and less empathetic towards Emma.

Chapter 14

Did Hardy Ever Regret Having Married Emma?

Hardy believed that men and women should be free to reject the formality of marriage and simply live together in a loving relationship if they so wished, and in this he was far ahead of his time.

Jude the Obscure was published in 1896. In April 1912, in a postscript written sixteen years after the book's publication, Hardy declared that 'The marriage laws' were: 'used in great part as the tragic machinery of the tale'; his own opinion being that 'a marriage should be dissolvable as soon as it becomes a cruelty to either of the parties - being then essentially and morally no marriage'.[1] What were these marriage laws that Hardy found so odious, and which were in force at the time when he composed *Jude the Obscure*?

In the book's Preface, Hardy stated that 'the scheme' for *Jude*:

> 'was jotted down in 1890, from notes made in 1887 and onwards, some of the circumstances being suggested by the death of a woman in the former year. The scenes were revisited in October 1892; the narrative was written in outline in 1892 and the spring of 1893, and at full length, as it now appears, from August 1893 onwards into the next year; the whole, with the exception of a few chapters, being in the hands of the publisher by the end of 1894.'

As regards the 'marriage laws', the Matrimonial Causes Act, 1857:

> 'was an Act of the Parliament of the United Kingdom. The Act reformed the law on divorce, moving litigation from the jurisdiction of the ecclesiastical courts to the civil courts, establishing a model of marriage based on contract rather than sacrament and widening the availability of divorce beyond

those who could afford to bring proceedings for annulment or to promote a private Bill.'

'Before the Act, divorce was governed by the ecclesiastical Court of Arches and the canon law of the Church of England. As such, it was not administered by the barristers, who practised in the common law courts, but by the "advocates" and "proctors" who practised civil law from Doctors' Commons, adding to the obscurity of the proceedings. Divorce allowing remarriage was de facto restricted to the very wealthy, as it demanded either a complex annulment process or a private bill, either, at great cost. The latter entailed sometimes lengthy debates about a couple's intimate marital relationship in public in the House of Commons.'

'The Act abolished Ecclesiastical jurisdiction regarding matrimonial matters, and for the first time made secular divorces possible (by court order). The Act created a new Court of Divorce and Matrimonial Causes and gave it jurisdiction to hear and decide civil actions for divorce. Further, it gave rights of audience both to common law barristers and civil law advocates, removing the advocates' previous monopoly in divorce proceedings.'

'The Act allowed legal separation by either husband or wife on grounds of adultery, cruelty, or desertion. Section 57 of the Act also enabled the parties to remarry after divorce …. It also altered the handling of adultery in English law: it abolished the crime of criminal conversation [a euphemism for sexual intercourse], but maintained the principle that "since a wife's adultery caused injury to the husband, it entitled him to claim compensation from the adulterer", implying that the wife was the property of the husband – not least because wives could not claim compensation from adulterous husbands. Compensation was no longer, however, paid to the cuckold, but to the court, and damages were not to be punitive or exemplary but purely to compensate a husband's loss of consortium (marital services) of his wife and damages to his reputation, honour, and family life.'

'The Act did not treat women's and men's grounds for divorce equally (mainly on the grounds that women's adultery was more serious because it introduced doubt as to the paternity of possible heirs). Thus, a husband could petition for divorce on the sole grounds that his wife had committed adultery, whereas a wife could only hope for a divorce based on adultery combined with

> other offences such as incest, cruelty, bigamy, desertion, etc. (or based on cruelty alone). The Act also required that a suit by a husband for adultery name the adulterer as a co-respondent, whereas this was not required in a suit by a wife.'[2]

Clearly, both before and after the passing of the 1857 Act, the obtaining of a divorce by financial means was quite beyond the means of 'ordinary folks'. In fact, as far as they were concerned, the only benefit to them was that divorce now became a secular matter, and the stranglehold of the Church's jurisdiction was removed. No wonder Hardy was so indignant!

Hardy expressed his views on marriage vicariously through the character of Sue Bridehead in *Jude the Obscure*. According to Chinese author Yu-hua Guo of Binzhou University, Binzhou, China:

> 'In Sue's definition, marriage should not be "only a sordid contract, based on material convenience in house holding, rating and taxing"[3] – a quote from the novel - but a "free union" based on temperaments.' In a "free union", said Guo, 'husband and wife are two equal independent individuals who have their own personality. There is no dreadful contract confining their relationship and they can undo it if it is difficult to continue.'[4]

In other words, marriage should be a reversible process, which begs the question, would Hardy have abandoned his marriage to Emma if that had been possible?

In his poem *Fetching Her* (published in 1922) Hardy described how he had set off for Cornwall where he met Emma for the first time; and yet the 'magic' that he had felt in those early times had swiftly evaporated, which left him wondering whether he would have been wiser not to have courted and married Emma at all. In the poem, Hardy refers to himself as 'My friend':

> An hour before the dawn,
> My friend,
> You lit your waiting bedside-lamp,
> Your breakfast-fire anon,
> And outing into the dark and damp
> You saddled, and set on.
>
> Thuswise, before the day,
> My friend,
> You sought her on her surfy shore,

To fetch her thence away
Unto your own new-builded door
For a staunch lifelong stay.

You said: 'It seems to be,
My friend,
That I were bringing to my place
The pure brine breeze, the sea,
The mews all her old sky and space,
In bringing her with me!'

But time is prompt to expugn,
My friend,
Such magic-minted conjurings:
The brought breeze fainted soon,
And then the sense of seamews' wings,
And the shore's sibilant tune.

So, it had been more due,
My friend,
Perhaps, had you not pulled this flower
From the craggy nook it knew,
And set it in an alien bower;
But left it where it grew!

Mew: the high-pitched cry of a gull.[5]
Limn: suffuse or highlight with a bright colour or light.

Similarly, in his poem *The Destined Pair* (published in 1928), Hardy wondered if it would have been better if he had never met Emma:

Two beings were drifting
Each one to the other:
No moment's veil-lifting
Or hint from another
Led either to weet
That the tracks of their feet
Were arcs that would meet.

One moved in a city,
And one in a village,
Where many a ditty

He tongued when at tillage
On dreams of a dim
Figure fancy would limn
That was viewless to him.

Would Fate have been kinder
To keep night between them? —
Had he failed to find her
And time never seen them
Unite so that, caught
In no burning love-thought,
She had faded unsought?

Weet: know.

Chapter 15

Despite all, Hardy, in Retrospect, Strove to See Emma in the Best Possible Light

On 29 January 1913 Hardy wrote to Florence Dugdale to say:

> 'I am getting through E's [Emma's] papers … It was, of course, sheer hallucination in her, poor thing, & not wilfulness ….'[1]

Flower, for his part, declared that despite all, Emma did have her lighter side:

> 'She became, by the slow growth of eccentricity, a distress on Hardy, and limned [highlighted[2]] to clearer view the darker shape of things in his mind. But she had her humours, conscious or otherwise. She remarked to Edmund Gosse one day:
>
> "I always beat my husband every morning".
> "Beat him!" exclaimed Gosse.
> "Yes, but only with a rolled-up copy of *The Times*".'[3]

Chapter 16

The Important Testimony of Alice ('Dolly') Gale

Is it possible to get a deeper insight into life in the Hardy household during the time leading up to and including Emma's death? Yes, because of the testimony of Alice Gale, nicknamed 'Dolly' who, as a 14-year-old, served as Emma's personal maid for a period of one year. Dolly subsequently married Canadian Tom Harvey, lived in Canada for 50 years, and raised a family of six children. Dolly gave two 'bird's eye views' of life in the Hardy household during her period of employment. She was first interviewed by publisher and local historian J. Stevens Cox on 18 June 1972, when she 'was visiting her daughter' who lived in London, Ontario, Canada; and Dolly was interviewed again in the early 1990s, this time by Welsh writer and poet Beryl Baigent, when she was a resident of a nursing home in Oxford, UK.

Dolly was born in Cheselbourne, ten miles north-east of Dorchester. Her father John Gale 'was a strict Anglican – so all the children would have surely been brought up to be honest and to tell the truth - which is important as far as her testimony in respect of the Hardy household is concerned - and a wheelwright by trade', married to Sarah Fanny (née Sparks), a volunteer midwife. Dolly grew up in Winterborne Muston and Piddlehinton (Hardy's 'Lower Longpuddle'), Dorset.[1] Said she:

> 'As soon as I left school in 1911, I watched the advertisement columns in *The Western Gazette* for a suitable job as I was very anxious to stand on my own feet. One day I saw an advertisement for [a] female help at Max Gate, the home of Mr and Mrs Thomas Hardy in Dorchester.'[2]
>
> 'Dolly recalls that her parents were not anxious for her to work at Max Gate as "Mr Hardy's morals were not considered to be of the best and my parents told me that I was to leave the home immediately if there was any questionable behaviour on his part toward me", she explained.[3] "A maid who had worked at Max Gate before I went there told me that a pretty made previous

> to her service had left because she was pregnant and had claimed that it was Mr Hardy's child. This frightened me to death, and I always tried to hide from him if I heard him coming."'[4]

Could this be true? Certainly, even as a youth, Hardy was an incurable romantic, though, owing to his shyness, the objects of his desire were often unaware of his interest in them. There is also strong anecdotal and circumstantial evidence that he fathered an illegitimate female child, Augusta Mary Humber, by a maid who was in his employ during the time that he and wife Emma lived at Sturminster Newton.[5]

Having been summoned for interview, said Dolly:

> 'I went on my bicycle from my home in Piddlehinton to Max Gate, a distance of some 6 miles. I knocked on the door and it was opened by a maid in uniform. She asked me into the hall and fetched Mrs Hardy, who invited me into the drawing room. She treated me in a very kindly way, and I immediately liked her. She explained to me that as her health was poor and she was getting weak she needed a personal help. Although my duties were not then precisely indicated, I understood from the conversation that if I accepted the job my duties would include carrying her breakfast and lunch to her bedroom on the third floor, running messages for her, being available for help night and day, and brushing her hair regularly. My uniform was to be a blue dress with a white collar. I was to have every other Sunday off and the weekly half day's holiday. I was to live at Max Gate and receive my board. I forget what the wages were. The terms were acceptable to me, and I gladly took the job.'
>
> 'Mrs Hardy permanently suffered from a pain in her back and constantly asked me to pat her back to give her a relief. I did not know, I do not know, what her ailment was. In those days you spoke when you were spoken to and did not ask personal questions.' (Gallstones, which were identified at post-mortem, not only cause pain in the upper abdomen, they can also cause referred pain radiating to the upper back.)
>
> 'There was always a fire burning in Mrs Hardy's bedroom on the attic floor where she habitually lived, and had her meals, only coming downstairs in the evenings for dinner. She and her husband had been "separated" for some time, but for appearances' sake still lived in the same house.'
>
> 'I was at Max Gate for about 12 months. Mrs Hardy lived entirely separate from Mr Hardy, and I never remember him

visiting her in her rooms or seeing her at all except at dinner the whole time I was there, and I never saw or heard them speak to each other. Mrs Hardy never talked to me about her husband who passed most of the day in his study. Nobody was allowed to enter this study except the housemaid to clear the fireplace and set the fire and Mr Hardy kept his eye on her the whole while. This irritated the housemaid. My impression was that Mr Hardy irritated most people and certainly all those who worked in the house. I never saw him smile. He only ever spoke to me if it was absolutely necessary and then in as few words as possible. Oh, he was a miserable old thing! I remember being asked by him on several occasions to fetch the mail and it usually included a letter from Macmillan [Hardy's publisher] with MACMILLAN on the envelope. Mr Hardy never had the manners to say "Thank you" when you fetched him anything.'[6] In fact, Dolly:

'was "scared" of Hardy and "ran like a frightened rabbit whenever [she] met him in the corridors of the house. "I despised him", she said with vehemence; "he had shifty eyes and [was] a wizen-up little man when I knew him."'

Wizened: shrivelled or wrinkled with age.[7]

'Dolly wore a blue dress with a white lace collar as her formal "uniform" in her "service" position.' In retrospect, she thought of herself as a "run-and-fetch gopher [dogsbody] more than a maid". Yet her duties also involved those of a companion to Mrs Hardy.'

'Dolly slept in an attic bedroom beside Emma and became jokingly known in her family as "Backstairs Dolly", as it was customary for the house staff to use only the stairs in the rear of the house.' While Dolly was employed at Max Gate:

'she was one of three servants along with a cook and housekeeper, both of whom were very good to her. Dolly's duties included taking up jugs of hot water to her mistress for washing in the mornings and carrying in her breakfast and lunch to the third-floor attic room. Sometimes Dolly would rub Emma's back when she was in great pain and "this seemed to give her relief". Dolly never asked, or expected to be told about the illness from which Emma suffered.'

'Even though Emma had been failing in health for some years, she still appeared in the dining room for dinner most

> nights. Emma was known to have a demanding attitude to her servants and scolded loudly if she was late with lunch. However, Dolly liked her a great deal and felt that Emma was a considerate mistress. "She never woke me in the night even though she was often in pain and I was right next door", she recalled. Dolly also brushed Emma's hair and rubbed her scalp, for twenty minutes every morning and most evenings.'[8]
>
> 'Mrs Hardy was mentally alert and I liked her very much, but I despised her husband. I slept on the same floor as Mrs Hardy so that she could call me quickly if I was needed during the night, but she never did call me. She was a most considerate and kindly employer. She liked me to attend church at Saint Peter's [Dorchester]. I went with the cook or the housemaid.'[9]
>
> 'Emma ... slept with her pampered cats and spent much of her time with Beau-Beau [her favourite] on her lap. "If the cat was out prowling at night, Mrs Hardy wouldn't settle down until I brought Beau-Beau in", Dolly remembered.'
>
> 'Dolly spoke about the "separation" between Thomas and Emma. "Mr and Mrs Hardy [had] lived separately for some time before I worked for them but they still lived in the same house together for appearance sake."'[10]

Dolly described Hardy's 'supercilious manner', which she 'disliked'. However, by contrast:

> 'Mrs Hardy gave me a chain purse as a present. I found her generous. I disliked Hardy so much since leaving Max Gate [that] I have rarely spoken of him.'[11]
>
> 'The Hardy household at Max Gate in 1912 were familiar with the woman who was to become Hardy's second wife. In fact, Dolly knew of her existence prior to her engagement and the fact that "Mr Hardy had a mistress in London" was one reason why her parents objected to Dolly applying for the position. Dolly remembers Florence Dugdale as being "a lovely lady with the most beautiful hair". Hardy's relationship with Miss Dugdale naturally caused some speculation among the household staff. They believed that every weekend, when Hardy went to London to consult his publisher, Macmillan, he was meeting his "girl friend".'
>
> 'During 1912, Dolly remembers that "once in a while, when there was a dinner party, Mrs Hardy would go down and sit at the table and act like a perfect hostess". Emma hosted a garden party in July of that year, and Dolly "served drinks" (possibly

his favourite cider to Mr Hardy) and recalls that it was a large gathering under the trees and included Miss Dugdale. Generally, Mrs Hardy appeared in the garden in a Bath chair which Dolly pushed. "Mrs Hardy liked me to take her for a walk and always chose a walk that was uphill. I wasn't very strong, and it was always hard work", Dolly notes. Emma also encouraged Dolly to attend services with her at Saint Peter's [Dorchester] and it was Sundays and holy days which presented some added interest in the otherwise humdrum days of life at Max Gate.'

'As Emma's health deteriorated during 1912, the bitter and open hostility between Mr and Mrs Hardy was evident to the staff. Dolly recalls that she never saw or heard the Hardys converse during her time at Max Gate, but Emma never complained or talked about her husband to her.'

'Dolly found Thomas Hardy to be "uncaring and cold" in his attitude to his wife, and this attitude generally consisted of "ignoring her". Emma's seventy-second birthday passed on 24 November with no ceremony, and although she was obviously weaker, she would not allow the doctor to examine her.'[12]

'On the morning of what was to be the day of Mrs Hardy's death, November 27, 1912, I entered her bedroom at about 8 a.m. She was moaning and terribly ill. Her appearance frightened me. She was so dreadfully drawn in her face. A great change had come over her since the previous evening. She did not complain but asked me to fetch Mr Hardy.'[13]

'"My mistress's appearance frightened me". In a weak voice Emma told Dolly "Fetch Tom, fetch Tom". No one was allowed to enter Hardy's new book-lined study on the second floor, except for the housekeeper who "cleared and set the fire". On this occasion Dolly entered his study unannounced.[14] 'I rushed downstairs to his study and asked him to come quickly as mistress was terribly ill and looked dreadful.[15] And yet Hardy seemed oblivious to the request to come "Right now" … and [he] was not a bit concerned.'[16]

'Hardy looked at me disdainfully and after several seconds said: "Your collar is crooked". He remained seated and carefully and methodically arranged the things on his desk as though that was more important than directly going to his wife. However, after a couple of minutes or so he followed me up to his wife's bedroom. It was apparent when he saw her that he was shocked by his wife's appearance as he then hurried to her bedside and said: "Emm, Emm, do you know me Emm" or "Emm, Emm,

> don't you know me, it's Tom" - I am not now certain which of these expressions he used. Mrs Hardy was too far gone to answer him and from then until she died in less than five minutes she did not speak. I was standing at the bottom of the bed during the whole of this time until she died, and I then left the room as I thought I was intruding. Within a few seconds Mr Hardy left the room and shut the door. I did not cry. I was too shocked. It was the first time I had seen death. Later that day the doctor and undertaker arrived.'[17]
>
> 'Even now [8 decades later!] Dolly still has apprehension in her voice as she recounts this incident. Dolly also remembers staring at a plaque on the desk rather than looking at Hardy's cold eyes. The words of the plaque are engraved forever on her mind and read: "Write, and with mine eyes I'll drink the words".' ('Write, my queen, And with mine eyes I'll drink the words you send': the words of Posthumus, from William Shakespeare's play *Cymbeline*, Act I, Scene I.)[18]
>
> 'I remember the coffin with Mrs Hardy lying in state at the foot of Mr Hardy's bed and it was then that a few friends came to pay their last respects. I don't remember the doctor visiting Mrs Hardy at any time while I was there. If he came it must have been on my day off. There was little grief shown when she died. I was shocked rather than being grieved as I had never been near death before. The maids were sent in charge of the cook to Genge's in Dorchester to buy new black outfits for the funeral and Hardy was very annoyed with cook as he thought the outfit should have been much less expensive.'
>
> 'The servants attended the funeral at Stinsford church. Dolly recalls that Emma's burial plot in Stinsford cemetery was "Under a greenwood tree, as he had written about in his [eponymous] novel". This novel became Dolly's favourite when she read Hardy's work many years later.'

Dolly completed her term of employment at Max Gate at the end of December 1912, when:

> 'her father came to take her home as her eldest sister had died in childbirth. Dolly returned home to Piddlehinton where she eventually met Tom Harvey, a Canadian who was visiting her [Dolly's] family along with her sister and brother-in-law who had just returned to England after living in Canada. "There was nothing to do around the little village of Piddlehinton except go

> for walks, so we got to know each other pretty well and decided to get married", Dolly explained. They were married on New Year's Day 1918, with her youngest sister, May, as bridesmaid, at the old Anglican church in Piddlehinton, a church whose graveyard dates back to the time when the first Gales were buried there. Dolly and her husband settled in Beaverton, Ontario where Tom found work as an electrician.' The couple had six children.
>
> 'The family moved to Ingersoll, Ontario at the outbreak of World War II. The two oldest children, Walter and May, served in the R.C.A.F. [Royal Canadian Air Force].'[19]

Following the death of Emma, said Dolly:

> 'Another matter that Mr Hardy attended to with urgency was to send a telegraphic message to Miss Florence Dugdale, who then moved into Max Gate with inordinate haste. I thought Hardy was paying too much attention to Miss Dugdale so soon after his wife's death. I thought he was trying to act too young - an old man acting "kittenish". I continued to work at Max Gate for about a month after Mrs Hardy's death and during most of that time I helped the housemaid. One day when we were making up the beds, as we shook out the sheets in Hardy's bedroom, there in his bed were two hairpins. The maid merely snorted, but when I realized the situation, I was shocked. At first, I had thought that Hardy and Miss Dugdale had changed beds during the night.'[20]

Of the authenticity of Dolly's testimony there can be no doubt, if only because of the intimate details it contains about the Hardy household.

Hardy's relationship with Florence

Whilst there is no proof that Hardy was having an affair with Florence while Emma was still alive, Dolly's testimony makes this extremely likely. Not only that, but Emma would probably have suspected, or heard rumours to the effect that this was the case, and she would also have been aware of her husband's track record of womanising.

Chapter 17

Hardy's Neglect of Emma

Who was responsible for the neglect which Emma suffered during the course of her final illness? This must surely be laid at the door of Hardy, who, unlike his wife, was in full command of his faculties. His dereliction of duty in ignoring the suffering of a fellow human being, and in particular of his wife, was unforgivable and it came as a shock to the family doctor, to Dolly, and doubtless of other members of the household.

Hardy's seeming indifference on hearing from Dolly that Emma was gravely ill, is an indication that he had long since given up on his wife. So, Dolly's account corroborates the statement of Dr Mann, who described the 'lack of attention' afforded to Emma by Hardy and her 'general discomfort'.

According to Florence, Emma did not consent to see a doctor until the day before her death,[1] and therefore, Hardy cannot be blamed for the delay in calling in medical advice. But why the delay? Perhaps because Emma feared that the doctor would recommend some sort of surgical procedure, which in those days would have been fraught with danger and carried a high mortality rate.

Hardy was capable of great love, as his poem *Middle-Age Enthusiasms* (published in 1898), which he dedicated to his sister Mary ('M. H.') indicates. In it, he revealed his love for her, in the knowledge that one day, as they were both mere mortals, their relationship must inevitably come to an end:

To M. H.

I

We passed where flag and flower
Signalled a jocund throng;
We said: 'Go to, the hour
Is apt!' - and joined the song;
And, kindling, laughed at life and care,
Although we knew no laugh lay there.

IV

'So sweet the place,' we said,
'Its tacit tales so dear,

Our thoughts, when breath has sped,
Will meet and mingle here!' …
'Words!' mused we. 'Passed the mortal door,
Our thoughts will reach this nook no more.'

Therefore, had circumstances been different, Hardy would surely have loved Emma all his life and with all his heart.

Chapter 18

Hardy and Time; the Afterlife; Einstein

1. Hardy's Preoccupation with Time

Hardy's poems and writings, composed after Emma's death but with her in mind, reveal that the concept of time was very much on his mind. If time could be reversed for example, then he and she could be reunited.

Hardy possessed no less than 9 volumes by English writer H. G. Wells in his library. However, *The Time Machine* (published in 1895) was not among them. Here, Wells popularised the concept of travel, whereby a person is able to travel backwards or forwards through time!

If only time would stand still!
On 14 July 1887 in his literary notebook, Hardy stated that 'if the world stood still at a felicitous moment there would be no sadness in it'. In other words, no new sad events would be experienced and therefore no new unhappy memories would be created.[1] Little did he know how sad he would be, after the death of Emma a quarter of a century later!

Felicitous: pleasing and fortunate.[2] Here, Hardy was undoubtedly thinking of the day when he and Emma first met – 7 March 1870 - as one of those moments!

Death and Immortality
In 2020 Trish Ferguson, Assistant Professor of English Literature at Liverpool Hope University, UK, attempted to ascertain Hardy's view on these two subjects, which were of the utmost interest to Hardy.[3]

Trish began by posing the vital question, put by Tess Durbeyfield to her husband Angel Clare in Hardy's novel *Tess of the d'Urbervilles*: 'Do you think we shall meet again after we are dead? I want to know'.[4] Whereupon Angel 'kissed her to avoid a reply at such a time'.

Time as a 'Construct' invented by human beings
Theoretical advances in physics, said Trish, had:

> 'led to an intellectual shift from understanding time as linear and teleological toward accepting time as a construct without any innate reality'.[5]
>
> 'Linear': progressing from one stage to another in a single series of steps.[6]
>
> 'Teleology': the doctrine of design and purpose in the material world.[7]
>
> 'Construct': an idea or theory containing various conceptual elements, typically one considered to be subjective and not based on empirical evidence.[8]
>
> 'Empirical': based on, concerned with, or verifiable by observation or experience rather than by pure logic.[9]

Here, Trish clearly had in mind the work of Albert Einstein, which will be discussed shortly. She continued:

> 'Rather than moving towards closure offered by traditional linear elegiac structures, Hardy's poems on mortality reflect the conflicting impulses that Seamus Perry [Professor of English Literature, Balliol College, Oxford, UK] sees as characteristic of the greatest elegiac poetry, which "doesn't exhibit merely a recuperative return to the word, but rather a kind of double-heartedness, which recognises the need to move on, while staying true to the dead".[10] Hardy was to reconcile the conflicting impulses that prompt elegiac utterance, I suggest, through philosophy based on non-linear conceptions of time.'[11]

'Elegy': a poem of serious reflection, typically a lament for the dead.[12]

'Lament': a passionate expression of grief or sorrow.[13]

Hardy and a longing to go back in time
'Hardy's poems of 1912-13 ... at times, seek to undermine the conception of time as linear and irreversible', said Trish. For example, in his poem *St Launce's Revisited* (published in 1914) he imagined returning to Cornwall and St Juliot where he first met Emma, and where he now anticipated seeing the old familiar faces, hers included:

Slip back, Time!
Yet again I am nearing
Castle and keep, uprearing
Gray, as in my prime.

At the inn
Smiling nigh, why is it
Not as on my visit
When hope and I were twin?

Groom and jade
Whom I found here, moulder;
Strange the tavern-holder,
Strange the tap-maid.

Here I hired
Horse and man for bearing
Me on my wayfaring
To the door desired.

Evening gloomed
As I journeyed forward
To the faces shoreward,
Till their dwelling loomed.

If again
Towards the Atlantic sea there
I should speed, they'd be there
Surely now as then? …

Castle: Launceston Castle. It was at Launceston that Hardy alighted from the train.

Jade: an old or worn-out horse.[14]

Tap-maid: barmaid.

Horse and man: Hardy made the rest of the journey to St Juliot by horse and carriage.

Till their dwelling loomed: i.e. St Julitta's Rectory and its occupants.

However, Hardy realized that only in his mind, and not in reality, could time be made to 'Slip back', as he concluded miserably:

Why waste thought,
When I know them vanished
Under earth; yea, banished
Ever into nought!

Nonetheless, said Hardy, he and the late Emma were free from the constraints of time

Hardy's 'Emma Poems' of 1912-13 (21 in all), published in 1914 in the collection *Satires of Circumstance*, 'subvert linear conceptions of time by presenting Emma as freed from temporality', said Trish.

Temporality: the state of existing within or having some relationship with time.[15]

For example, in his poem *After a Journey*, Hardy imagined that the late Emma had guided to him to Cornwall, where they had once been happy. But time was an irrelevance, because he imagined her as she was then, and he himself as unchanged since those days:

III
I see what you are doing: you are leading me on
To the spots we knew when we haunted here together,
The waterfall, above which the mist-bow shone
At the then fair hour in the then fair weather,
And the cave just under, with a voice still so hollow
That it seems to call out to me from forty years ago,
When you were all aglow,
And not the thin ghost that I now frailly follow!

Ghost: an apparition of a dead person which is believed to appear or become manifest to the living, typically as a nebulous image.[16]

Nebulous: in the form of a cloud or haze.[17]

And the poem concludes:

Trust me, I mind not, though Life lours,
The bringing me here; nay, bring me here again!
I am just the same as when
Our days were a joy, and our paths through flowers.

'Mist-bow': rainbow.
'Lour': look angry or sullen; scowl.[18]

In Hardy's imagination, only by rejecting the traditional, linear notion of time could he leapfrog backwards and reconnect with Emma.

Hardy, for 'a moment', believed that the sound of a voice (i.e. Emma's!), or a kiss (from Emma, of course!) could transcend time
Transcendent: beyond or above the range of normal or physical human experience. Transcendental: relating to a spiritual realm. [19]

For example, in his poem *In a Whispering Gallery* (published in 1917), Hardy raises the possibility of a voice echoing down the years, and thus offering the prospect of immortality:

That whisper takes the voice
Of a Spirit, speaking to me,
Close, but invisible,
And throws me under a spell
At the kindling vision it brings;
And for a moment I rejoice,
And believe in transcendent things
That would make of this muddy earth
A spot for the splendid birth
Of everlasting lives,
Whereto no night arrives;
And this gaunt gray gallery
A tabernacle of worth
On this drab-aired afternoon,
When you can barely see
Across its hazed lacune
If opposite aught there be
Of fleshed humanity
Wherewith I may commune;
Or if the voice so near
Be a soul's voice floating here.

Likewise, in his poem *A Kiss* (also published in 1917), he imagined that the eponymous kiss – presumably one that he had once given or received from Emma - may have continued its existence in the 'ether'.[20]

By a wall the stranger now calls his,
Was born of old a particular kiss,
Without forethought in its genesis;
Which in a trice took wing on the air.
And where that spot is nothing shows:

There ivy calmly grows,
And no one knows
What a birth was there.

That kiss is gone where none can tell -
Not even those who felt its spell:
It cannot have died; that know we well.
Somewhere it pursues its flight,
One of a long procession of sounds
Travelling aethereal rounds
Far from earth's bounds
In the infinite.

Ethereal (or 'Aethereal'): extremely delicate and light in a way that seems not to be of this world.[21]

'Infinite': limitless or endless in space, extent, or size; impossible to measure or calculate.[22]

2. Hardy, Emma, and the 'Afterlife'

Hardy was preoccupied with the idea of the 'Afterlife', even prior to the death of Emma, but Emma's death gave his investigations into that concept even more impetus. For example, in 1901, a decade prior to her death, Hardy declared in respect of spiritualism, that:

> 'he would give ten years of his life to see "an authentic indubitable spectre", but he struggled to accept the idea of an afterlife without material proof.'[1]

Spiritualism: a system of belief or religious practice based on supposed communication with the spirits of the dead, especially through mediums.[2]

Medium: a person claiming to be in contact with the spirits of the dead and to communicate between the dead and the living.[3]

Spectre: a visible disembodied spirit: ghost.[4]

In other words, for Hardy, his beliefs had to be evidence-based.

In Hardy's song '*As Twere To-night*' (published in 1922) his spirits soared as a vision – again undoubtedly that of Emma - appeared to him. The poem, said Trish, seemed 'to promise the conservation of past times in a future afterlife'.[5]

As 'twere to-night, in the brief space
Of a far eventime,
My spirit rang achime
At vision of a girl of grace;
As 'twere to-night, in the brief space
Of a far eventime.

As 'twere at noontide of to-morrow
I airily walked and talked,
And wondered as I walked
What it could mean, this soar from sorrow;
As 'twere at noontide of to-morrow
I airily walked and talked.

As 'twere at waning of this week
Broke a new life on me;
Trancings of bliss to be
In some dim dear land soon to seek;
As 'twere at waning of this week
Broke a new life on me!

A girl of grace: this, of course, is Emma, with whom he imagined being reunited in a blissful joint reunion.

'Achime': chiming.
'Broke': commenced.
'Trancings': daydreams.
'Some dim dear land': presumably the land of the afterlife.

In Hardy's poem *When Dead* (published in 1925), said Trish, 'rather than suggesting an afterlife in heaven or posthumous reconciliation', Hardy 'posits a posthumous existence suggestive of McTaggart's timeless immortality conceived of as "the Vast"'.

'Posit': put forward as a fact or as a basis for argument.[6]

McTaggart, John E.: English idealist and metaphysician (1866-1925).

'The Vast': an immense space.[7]

And in the 'Vast', Hardy anticipated being reunited with Emma:

It will be much better when
I am under the bough;

I shall be more myself, Dear, then,
Than I am now.

No sign of querulousness
To wear you out
Shall I show there: strivings and stress
Be quite without.

This fleeting life-brief blight
Will have gone past
When I resume my old and right
Place in the Vast.

And when you come to me
To show you true.
Doubt not I shall infallibly
Be waiting you.

In his poem '*So, Time*' (published in 1925), Hardy expressed the view that the notion of time was irrelevant, because he believed that even though those who have gone before had died, their 'being' continued to exist in the 'Vast'.

    So, Time,
    Royal, sublime;
Heretofore held to be
Master and enemy,
Thief of my Love's adornings,
Despoiling her to scornings:—
The sound philosopher
Now sets him to aver
    You are nought
    But a thought
Without reality.

'Time' had torn Emma from him, and now Hardy takes his revenge by dismissing time as irrelevant.

    Young, old,
    Passioned, cold,
All the loved-lost thus
Are beings continuous,
In dateless dure abiding,

Over the present striding
With placid permanence
That knows not transience:
　　Firm in the Vast,
　　First, last;
Afar, yet close to us.

3. Albert Einstein: for Hardy, the Answer to a Prayer?

In respect of Hardy's longing to be in some way reunited with Emma, the words 'frantic', 'obsessed', 'driven', 'desperate' come to mind. But did he have any grounds for hope? Yes, because the work of German-Jewish mathematician and physicist Albert Einstein (1879-1955) convinced him that such a reunification might indeed be possible.

Said US astrophysicist and science writer Michael Schirber:

> 'Albert Einstein was famous for many things, but his greatest brainchild is the theory of relativity. It forever changed our understanding of space and time. Space and time are relative.' Furthermore, 'Different viewers will see the timing and spacing of events differently.'

Relativity: the dependence of various physical phenomena on relative motion of the observer and the observed objects, especially regarding the nature and behaviour of light, space, time, and gravity.[1]

In 1905, Einstein's *The Special Theory of Relativity* was published in the German physics journal *Annalen der Physik*. This was followed in 1916, by Einstein's scientific paper 'Die Grundlage der Allgemeinen Relativitatstheorie', translated as 'The Foundation of the General Theory of Relativity', which was published in the same journal.

Finally, in 1920, Einstein's *Relativity: The Special and the General Theory: A Popular Exposition* became available in English translation, and it may come as a surprise that Hardy acquired a copy of this volume for his library.[2]

Did Hardy study the work? Yes, of this there is no doubt. In his own handwriting, on the title page he wrote his name; on page 19 in the text, he underlined the word 'relativity'; on page 111, in the margin, he wrote the words 'globe' and 'surface' followed by a question mark '?'.

On page 27 of *Relativity*, the first paragraph reads as follows:

> 'Now before the advent of the theory of relativity it had always tacitly been assumed in physics that the statement of

> time had an absolute significance, *i.e.* that it is independent of the state of motion of the body of reference. But we have just seen that this assumption is incompatible with the most natural definition of simultaneity; if we discard this assumption, then the conflict between the law of the propagation of light *in vacuo* and the principle of relativity (developed in Section VII) disappears.'

The second paragraph begins, 'We were led to that conflict by the considerations of Section VI, which are no longer tenable.' Einstein then proceeded to give as an example, an observer in a moving railway carriage, and another observer observing that carriage while standing on the railway platform, to illustrate relativity. This deduction by Einstein, that time is not an absolute phenomenon, clearly had some significance for Hardy, because in the right-hand margin beside the second paragraph, he drew a vertical line.

Hardy was fascinated by the work, said Florence of her husband, and he 'ponders over Einstein's Theory of Relativity in the night'.[3] Not only that, but Hardy mentioned Einstein specifically in a letter and in a poem, and alluded to him in his notebook. For example, in a letter to John McTaggart dated 31 December 1919, Hardy wrote:

> 'I have of late been getting out of patience, if not with philosophers, with men of science. You probably, or I shd [should] say certainly, have grasped with ease all that Einstein has been telling us, which is more than I have done. Really after what he says the universe seems to be getting too comic for words.' And Hardy described himself as 'thinking queerly of time and space'.[4]

Hardy may be forgiven for understanding only incompletely the works of Einstein, arguably the cleverest human being that has ever lived!

In his notebook entry dated 10 June 1923, Hardy stated as follows:

> 'Relativity. That things & events always were, are, & will be (e.g. Emma, Mother and Father are living still in the past).'[5]

Referring to Hardy's 'post-Einstein poems' Trish stated that 'relativity undoes death, thus effacing the need for elegiac utterance'.[6] One such poem by Hardy is *The Absolute Explains* (published in 1925).

'Absolute': that which exists without being dependent on anything else: the ultimate reality.[7]

This poem is of great significance because it reflects Hardy's way of thinking in respect of the matter that was always paramount in his mind; the possibility that, in some form or other, Emma was still alive, even though she had died 13 years previously.

I
"O no," said It: "her lifedoings
Time's touch hath not destroyed:
They lie their length, with the throbbing things
Akin them, down the Void,
Live, unalloyed.

Who was 'It'? Apparently, 'It' was the conveyer of the message that Hardy wished to hear. Could it be the voice of Einstein himself, conveying the message which Hardy believed was contained in the great scientist's Theory of Relativity, which he now applied to Emma.

'Void': containing nothing; not inhabited.[8]

Hardy evidently interpreted this to mean that Emma's life's work continued to exist, in a place devoid of consciousness. But had he interpreted the message correctly? This will be discussed shortly.

II

"Know, Time is toothless, seen all through;
The Present, that men but see,
Is phasmal: since in a sane purview
All things are shaped to be
Eternally.

'Phasm': an apparition; phantom.[9]
'Apparition': a ghost or ghostlike image of a person.[10]
'Phantom': a ghost; a figment of the imagination.[11]
'Sane purview': reasonable or sensible range of experience or thought.[12]
'Shaped': made.[13]
'Eternal': lasting or existing forever; without end.[14]

In other words, whereas on the one hand time is associated with decay and death, on the other 'all things', presumably including all living things, endure in some form or other.

III
"Your "Now" is just a gleam, a glide
Across your gazing sense:
With me, "Past", "Future", ever abide:
They come not, go not, whence
They are never hence.

For Hardy, the past, present, and future are one.

VI
— Thus It: who straightway opened then
The vista called the Past,
Wherein were seen, as fair as when
They seemed they could not last,
Small things and vast.

Here, the 'It' which gave Hardy access to the past – or so he thought - may well have been Einstein! And the 'small things and vast', which were as beautiful as ever, would surely have included Emma!

XI
"Here you see her who, by these laws
You learn of, still shines on,
As pleasing-pure as erst she was,
Though you think she lies yon,
Graved, glow all gone.

Surely the 'laws' to which Hardy referred were the theories of Einstein, who he believed he had to thank for preserving Emma in all her glory.

XVI
"So thus doth Being's length transcend
Time's ancient regal claim
To see all lengths begin and end.
'The Fourth Dimension' fame
Bruits as its name."

'Bruits': spreads widely.[15]

Here, Hardy's mention of the 'Fourth Dimension', which Einstein had referred to in Chapter XVII of his *Special Theory of Relativity*, suggests that yes, Hardy, who possessed a copy of Einstein's book, had read this work. Not only that, the poem implies that the lives of human beings – Emma's included of course - transcend time.

The above poem presents something of a paradox. Hardy on the one hand appears to interpret Einstein's Theory of Relativity to mean that when human life becomes extinct in a physical sense, nonetheless it is immutable (unchanging over time[16]) in a transcendent sense, i.e. Emma lives on per se (i.e. intrinsically). But on the other hand, he implies that her 'continuity' lives on in him - i.e. in his (and perhaps in no one else's) memory.

Organic: relating to or derived from living matter.[17]

Finally, in verse VIII of his poem *Drinking Song*, Hardy referred specifically to Einstein:

And now comes Einstein with a notion —
Not yet quite clear
To many here —
That's there's no time, no space, no motion,
Nor rathe nor late,
Nor square nor straight,
But just a sort of bending-ocean.

'Rathe': blooming or ripening (of flowers or fruit) early in the year.

'Bending-ocean': perhaps this phrase was suggested to Hardy by Einstein's reference to 'curved space' in Chapter XXXI of his *General Theory of Relativity*.

But again, was Hardy correct in interpreting Einstein's message to mean that there is 'no time, no space, no motion'? This will be discussed shortly.

4. Einstein and Michele Besso

In 1955 an incident occurred, which appeared to shed light on Einstein's beliefs in regard to death and the 'afterlife'.

Michele Besso, born on 25 May 1873, was a Swiss-Italian engineer and close friend of Einstein. This was during Einstein's years at the Swiss Federal Polytechnic in Zurich, Switzerland from 1896, when he was aged 17, until 1900, and during his years as assistant examiner at the patent office in Bern from 1902 to 1909.

Following Besso's death on 15 March 1955, Einstein sent a letter of condolence to the Besso family. Dated 21 March, the letter concluded with the following paragraph:

'Now he [Besso] has again preceded me a little in parting from this strange world. This has no importance. For people like us

> who believe in physics, the separation between past, present, and future has only the importance of an admittedly tenacious illusion.' Einstein, Albert (1879-1955). Autograph letter signed ('A. Einstein') to Michele Besso's son, Vero, and sister, Bice Rusconi.[1]

These words were written by the great scientist 27 years after the death of Hardy, but what do they mean? That the passage of time is a continuous process – a 'continuum' - and that separating it into past, present, and future is merely an illusion.

> 'Continuum': a continuous sequence in which adjacent elements are not perceptibly different from each other but the extremes are quite distinct.[2]

In his book *The General Theory of Relativity*, Einstein stated that:

> 'certain co-ordinate systems are given preference for the description of the four-dimensional space-time continuum.'[3]

Four-dimensional: having four dimensions, typically the three dimensions of space (length, breadth, and depth), plus time.[4]

Space-time: the concepts of time and three-dimension space regarded as fused in a four-dimensional continuum.[5]

A three-dimensional (3D) coordinate system is formed by the intersection of three axes that are perpendicular to each other at the origin. The three axes are labelled the x-axis, y-axis, and the z-axis. The coordinate system is used to specify the position of a point in three-dimensional space. The four co-ordinates … which determine an event', said Einstein, are 'x', 'y', 'z', and 't' representing time.[6]

Einstein himself died a month later, on 18 April 1955.

5. Einstein: Hardy's Huge Misinterpretation

Religion having failed to provide Hardy with an answer, as far as the possibility of an afterlife was concerned, had turned his attention to science.

The famous mathematician and physicist Albert Einstein, in his book on the subject of 'Relativity', described time and space as a 'Continuum' – continuous sequence – and the notion of 'past', 'present', and 'future' simply as an illusion.

When Einstein stated that time was a 'Continuum', Hardy took this to mean that time was an irrelevance, that the past, present, and future were all as one, and that therefore his late family and late friends continued to exist. After all if, as Hardy stated under the heading 'Relativity': that 'things & events always were, are, & will be (e.g. Emma, Mother and Father are living still in the past)', then surely when he himself died, *he too* would be still living in the past – i.e. he would be able to join them and be reunited with them. But did Einstein view matters in the same light? The answer is no.

Unfortunately for Hardy, he had misinterpreted the work of Einstein, who, when he spoke of a 'Continuum', was in fact referring, not to living things but to the inorganic world of stars, planets, etcetera. Because clearly for plants and animals, time is not a continuum; over time, one species may evolve, for example, and another may become extinct.

On 5 February 1921, almost 7 years prior to Hardy's death, Einstein made the following pronouncement:

> 'The mystical trend of our time, which shows itself particularly in the rampant growth of the so-called Theosophy and Spiritualism, is for me no more than a symptom of weakness and confusion. Since our inner experiences consist of reproductions, and combinations of sensory impressions, the concept of a soul without a body seem to me to be empty and devoid of meaning.'[1]

Theosophy: any number of philosophies maintaining that a knowledge of God may be achieved through spiritual ecstasy, direct intuition, or special individual relations, especially the movement founded in 1875 as the Theosophical Society by Helena Blavatsky and Henry Steel Olcott.[2]

Whether or not Hardy was aware of these views of Einstein's is not known.

Was Einstein *in any sense* religious? In 1934, 16 years after Hardy's death, in his book *Albert Einstein: The World as I See It*, Einstein, stated:

> 'A knowledge of the existence of something we cannot penetrate, of the manifestations of the profoundest reason and the most radiant beauty, which are only accessible to our reason in their most elementary forms – it is this knowledge and this emotion that constitute the truly religious attitude, in this sense, and in this alone, I am a deeply religious man. [However] I cannot conceive of a God who rewards and punishes his creatures, or has a will of the type of which we are conscious in ourselves. An

individual who should survive his physical death is also beyond my comprehension, nor do I wish it otherwise, such notions are for the fears or absurd egoism of feeble souls. Enough for me the mystery of the eternity of life, and the inkling of the marvellous structure of reality, together with the single-handed endeavour to comprehend a portion, be it never so tiny, of the reason that manifests itself in nature.'[3]

Finally, 25 years after Hardy's death, in a reply to a letter sent to him on 17 July 1953, Einstein wrote:

> 'I do not believe in immortality of the individual, and I consider ethics to be an exclusively human concern with no superhuman authority behind it.'[4]

Therefore, despite his words of comfort to the family of Michele Besso 2 years later in March 1955, in which he described the 'past, present and future' as merely 'an admittedly tenacious illusion', Einstein did not believe in an afterlife, and was scornful of those who did. And, therefore, whatever inferences Hardy had drawn from Einstein's *Theory of Relativity*, it is clear that the former had drawn the wrong conclusion.

But Hardy was desperate to reunite with Emma, and as such was likely to grasp at any straws.

6. Hardy's Final Days: Four Important Poems

1. By Hardy himself

In mid-December 1927, said Florence, as his earthy journey was drawing to a close, Hardy 'was anxious that a poem he had written, *Christmas in the Elgin Room* (published in 1928) should be copied and sent to *The Times*'.[1]

Hardy was a frequent visitor to the British Museum, where the 'Elgin Marbles' were on display.

Elgin Marbles: a collection of classical Greek marble sculptures and architectural fragments, chiefly from the Parthenon in Athens, brought to England by the diplomat and art connoisseur Thomas Bruce (1766-1841), the 7th Earl of Elgin.[2] The marbles were created in the 5th century BCE and are thought to depict gods and goddesses of Greece in the 13th century BCE.

In the poem, Hardy imagines the marble gods pondering over how Christianity supplanted the mythology of Greece of ancient times.

"WHAT is the noise that shakes the night,
And seems to soar to the Pole-star height?"
– "Christmas bells,
The watchman tells
Who walks this hall that blears us captives with
its blight."

"And what, then, mean such clangs, so clear?"
"— 'Tis said to have been a day of cheer,
And source of grace
To the human race
Long ere their woven sails winged us to exile
here.

"We are those whom Christmas overthrew
Some centuries after Pheidias knew
How to shape us
And bedrape us
And to set us in Athena's temple for men's view.

"O it is sad now we are sold —
We gods! for Borean people's gold,
And brought to the gloom
Of this gaunt room
Which sunlight shuns, and sweet Aurore but
enters cold.

"For all these bells, would I were still
Radiant as on Athenai's Hill."
- "And I, and I ! "
The others sigh,
"Before this Christ was known, and we had men's
good will."

Here, the gods are clearly expressing the desire to put the clock back to the pre-Christian era. Instead, they are obliged to listen to the sound of church bells at Christmas time!

Thereat old Helios could but nod,
Throbbed, too, the Ilissus River-god,
And the torsos there

Of deities fair,
Whose limbs were shards beneath some Acropolitan
clod:

Dementer too, Poseidon hoar,
Persephone, and many more
Of Zeus' high breed, —
All loth to heed
What the bells sang that night which shook them to
the core.

2. By Walter de la Mare (1873-1956)
In early January 1928, 'in the middle of one night', said Florence, Hardy 'asked his wife [i.e. her] to read aloud to him *The Listeners* by Walter de La Mere:[3]

'Is there anybody there?' said the Traveller,
Knocking on the moonlit door;
And his horse in the silence champed the grasses
Of the forest's ferny floor:
And a bird flew up out of the turret,
Above the Traveller's head:
And he smote upon the door again a second time;
'Is there anybody there?' he said.
But no one descended to the Traveller;
No head from the leaf-fringed sill
Leaned over and looked into his grey eyes,
Where he stood perplexed and still.
But only a host of phantom listeners
That dwelt in the lone house then
Stood listening in the quiet of the moonlight
To that voice from the world of men:
Stood thronging the faint moonbeams on the dark
stair,
That goes down to the empty hall,
Hearkening in an air stirred and shaken
By the lonely Traveller's call.
And he felt in his heart their strangeness,
Their stillness answering his cry,
While his horse moved, cropping the dark turf,
'Neath the starred and leafy sky;
For he suddenly smote on the door, even
Louder, and lifted his head:—

Tell them I came, and no one answered,
 That I kept my word,' he said.
Never the least stir made the listeners,
 Though every word he spake
Fell echoing through the shadowiness of the still
house
 From the one man left awake:
Ay, they heard his foot upon the stirrup,
 And the sound of iron on stone,
And how the silence surged softly backward,
 When the plunging hoofs were gone.

What is the meaning of this poem. It appears that 'the Traveller' is a living person who is attempting, unsuccessfully, to make contact with 'phantoms' – i.e. the souls of the dead - who are aware of his presence but fail to respond to him.

In desperation, he knocks at their door three times. He has a sense of being alone; he feels desolate. He cannot do anything about the situation, but he has done his best and can do no more.

By 'I kept my word', the traveller means that he will not forget them, even though he feels it his duty to reconnect with them. If this is the case, then Walter de la Mare's poem The Traveller would surely resonate with Hardy!

3. By Robert Browning (1812-1889)
In the evening of 10 January 1928, said Florence, Hardy 'asked that Robert Browning's poem *Rabbi Ben Ezra* should be read aloud to him':[4] The poem begins as follows:

Grow old along with me!
The best is yet to be,
The last of life, for which the first was made:
Our times are in His hand
Who saith "A whole I planned,
Youth shows but half; trust God: see all, nor be afraid!"

The meaning of this verse? That man's destiny is in the hands of God.

VI
Then, welcome each rebuff
That turns earth's smoothness rough,
Each sting that bids nor sit nor stand but go!
Be our joys three-parts pain!

Strive, and hold cheap the strain;
Learn, nor account the pang; dare, never grudge the throe!

In other words, the struggle may be painful, but we must persevere and not complain.

XXVI
Ay, note that Potter's wheel,
That metaphor! and feel
Why time spins fast, why passive lies our clay, —
Thou, to whom fools propound,
When the wine makes its round,
"Since life fleets, all is change; the Past gone, seize to-day!"

This says, live for the moment!

XXXII
So, take and use Thy work:
Amend what flaws may lurk,
What strain o' the stuff, what warpings past the aim!
My times be in Thy hand!
Perfect the cup as planned!
Let age approve of youth, and death complete the same!

According to Dr Ejaz Alam, Associate Professor and Head of English at Maulana Mazharul Haque Arabic and Persian University, Patna, Bihar, India:

> 'Through the metaphor of the potter and the pitcher, Browning explains God's plan for man. God is the potter who is shaping the clay (man) on the wheel of life. He is shaping man by giving him pain and suffering and failure. All this is meant to strengthen his character so that he emerges a strong man. This is also his explanation for the imperfection we see around us. The world is imperfect because God has made it so to try man. Thus, behind imperfect man and the imperfect world is perfect God who has a plan. Man has only to submit to the plan to know his place in the scheme of things. Once the pitcher is shaped, it is ready for use by the Gods. The soul has been purified by suffering and now it is ready for its journey which comes after death.'[5]

Although Hardy was an atheist as far as the Christian God was concerned, he did believe in predestiny, in other words, that God – or the 'Immanent Doer', to use his term, 'has a plan'.

4. By Hakim Omar Khayyám (1048-1131)

'As it grew dusk' on the evening of 11 January 1928, Hardy asked Florence 'to repeat to him a verse from the Rubdiydt of Omar Khayyám':[6]

Oh, Thou, who Man of baser Earth didst make,
And ev'n with Paradise devise the Snake:
For all the Sin wherewith the Face of Man
Is blacken'd – Man's forgiveness give - and take!

'Rubdiydt': Rubaiyat -a verse form consisting of four-line stanzas.

The author of the poem was Persian mathematician, astronomer, and poet in the Sufi tradition Hakim Omar Khayyám and the text was translated from the Persian (Farsi) by English poet and writer Edward FitzGerald (1809 - 1883).

Sufi: a mystical sect of Islam founded in the 8th century.

Paradise: from 'Paradis', Persian for an enclosed garden.

Snake: a symbol of evil.

In Persian, Ahura Mazda was the creator deity.

Just as God must forgive man, so man must forgive God. This notion would have resonating strongly with Hardy!

Hardy died on that same evening of 11 January 1928.

Summary

These four poems were among the last that Hardy read, or had read to him, during his earthly life. Why did they have a special significance for him?

Christmas in the Elgin Room: how different religions may come and go.

The Listeners: How it is impossible for a living person to make contact with the dead, no matter how hard he tries.

Rabbi Ben Ezra: it is God's will for man to suffer, and once his soul has been purified, the afterlife awaits.

Rubaiyat of Omar Khayyám: in regard to man's relationship with God, forgiveness must be a two-way process!

In the light of this, what was going through Hardy's mind? As he hovered between belief and unbelief, the possibility that yes, perhaps there was a 'God' after all?

Chapter 19

Hardy's Later Years

1. Further Honours for Hardy

A 'Poets' Tribute' book was compiled and presented to Hardy in 1919, on the occasion of his 79th birthday, by war poet, writer, and soldier Siegfried Sassoon. It was signed by forty-three poets, including Edmund Blunden, Robert Graves, D. H. Lawrence, Rudyard Kipling, and Sassoon himself, and contained handwritten poems in which they each showed their respect for the great man.[1]

On 20 July 1923, wrote Florence, the Prince of Wales – the future King Edward VIII:

> 'paid a visit to Dorchester to open the new Drill Hall for the Dorset Territorials [Territorial Army Infantry Regiment], and Hardy was invited to meet him there, and to drive back to Max Gate where the Prince and the party accompanying him were to lunch. It was a hot day, and the whole episode might well have proved fatiguing and irksome to a man of Hardy's years and retiring nature but owing to the thoughtfulness of the Prince and his simple and friendly manner, all passed off pleasantly.'
>
> 'At lunch, beside the Prince and the Hardys, there were present Lord Shaftesbury [Lord Steward of the Royal Household], Admiral Sir Lionel Halsey [the Prince's equerry], Sir Godfrey Thomas [the Prince's Private Secretary], Mr (afterwards Sir) Walter Peacock [Liberal politician and barrister], and Messrs Proudfoot and Wilson, the Duchy Stewards [Stewards of the Duchy of Lancaster, a portfolio of land, property, and assets owned by the sovereign].'
>
> 'The Prince had a friendly talk with Hardy in the garden, before leaving to visit certain Duchy farms in Dorchester: the main characteristic of the visit was its easy informality.'[2]

Meanwhile, there followed from Hardy a collection of short stories entitled *A Changed Man and Other Tales* (1913); and another collection of poems entitled *Satires of Circumstance* (poetry anthology, 1914).

2. Marriage to Florence Dugdale (10 February 1914)

On 10 February 1914, Hardy married Florence Emily Dugdale. In a letter dated 24 February 1914 to a former pupil of hers, Harold Barlow, who was currently working in Africa, Florence wrote:

> 'Perhaps you have read, if you have the English papers, that I am now the proud and very happy wife of the greatest living English writer - Thomas Hardy. Although he is so much older than myself it is a genuine love match - on my part, at least, for I suppose I ought not to speak for him. At any rate I know I have for a husband one of the kindest, most humane men in the world.'[1]

What a contrast Florence's admiring and appreciative view of Hardy was to that of his first wife Emma, who had poured heaps of vitriol on her husband's head and judged herself to be the greater writer of the two!

In June 1916, wrote Florence, Hardy:

> 'paid a visit with his wife and remaining sister [Kate] to a house he had never entered for forty years. This was Riverside Villa, Sturminster Newton - the first he had furnished after his first marriage, and in which he had written *The Return of the Native*.'

In September 1916, said Florence, she and Hardy:

> 'set out by train for Cornwall, breaking the journey at Launceston. Thence they went on to Camelford, Boscastle, and St Juliot, to see if Hardy's design and inscription for the [memorial] tablet in the church had been properly carried out and erected.'[2]

At Tintagel church, said Hardy, he was particularly interested in the nave, which Emma 'had sketched in watercolours when she was a young woman before it was "restored" ...'[3] It was no accident that Hardy, who detested the current vogue for restoration, had put the word 'restored' in parenthesis!

On 9 December 1916 Florence described a visit to St Julitta's Rectory, where she and Hardy 'had tea ... with the very nice Rector [the Reverend John H. Dickinson] & his sister'. She also described exploring King Arthur's castle where the couple 'lay for an hour or so, on the grass, in the sunshine, with sheep nibbling around us, & no other living thing – while cliffs & greenyblue sea & white surf seemed hundreds of feet below'.[4] In other words this time, unlike on the first occasion, Florence, appears to have enjoyed her visit to Cornwall as, apparently, did Hardy!

The revisiting by Hardy of places which he had known and loved because of their association with Emma indicates that the memory of his late wife remained forever dear to his heart.

On 24 May 1922, said Florence:

> 'Hardy motored to Sturminster Newton to call at the [aforementioned] house where he spent some of the early years of his first marriage and where he wrote *The Return of the Native*.'[5]

27 November 1927, said Florence, was:

> 'The fifteenth anniversary of the death of Emma Lavinia Hardy; Thursday was the anniversary of the death of Mary, his older sister. For two or three days he has been wearing a black hat as a token of mourning and carries a black walking stick that belonged to his first wife, all strangely moving.'

3. What Florence had Really Thought of Emma

On 16 January 1913, the month after Emma's death, Florence, in a lengthy letter to Edward Clodd, wrote of Hardy as follows:

> 'His life here is *lonely* beyond words, & he spends his evenings in reading & re-reading voluminous diaries that Mrs H. [the late Emma] has kept from the time of their marriage. Nothing could be worse for him. He reads the comments upon himself - bitter denunciations, beginning about 1891 [17 years after their marriage] & continuing until within a day or two of her death - & I think he will end by *believing* them.' In other words, Florence considered Emma's comments to be preposterous and without foundation.

Despite this, however, Florence did all in her power to make Hardy's life bearable. Said she: 'I read aloud to him every evening after dinner, until eleven o'clock & take as much care of him as I possibly can'. And in a postscript to her letter to Clodd, she added:

> 'Of course nothing could be more lonely than the life he used to lead - long evenings spent alone in his study, insult & abuse his only enlivenment. It sounds cruel to write like that, & in atrocious taste, but truth is truth, after all'.[1]

On 30 January 1913 Florence, writing from her home at Enfield, Middlesex, where her father was a headmaster, told Clodd that she had received a letter that day from Hardy, who had informed her that he was 'getting through E's papers'. Speaking of Emma's abuse of him, Hardy declared: 'It was, of course, sheer hallucination in her, poor thing, & not wilfulness!' Characteristically, Hardy was protective towards Emma but his opinion was certainly not shared by Florence. In fact, so annoyed did she become that she told Clodd: 'I feel as if I can hardly keep back my true opinion much longer'.[2]

Florence, who was exasperated by the fact that Hardy was still in denial about his disastrous marriage to Emma said with unveiled sarcasm:

> 'On Thursday he started to Plymouth to find a grave of Mrs H's [Emma's] father [John Attersoll Gifford] (- that amiable gentleman who wrote to him as "a low-born churl who has presumed to marry into *my* family"). 'Today he goes to Cornwall, to St Juliot's [Julitta's] Rectory, where he first met his "late, espousèd saint" [a quotation from 17th century poet and historian John Milton's Sonnet XXII], forty-three years ago this very week.' Florence, in fact, accompanied him on this visit.
>
> 'However, as his youngest sister [Kate] sensibly observes, "so long as he doesn't pick up another Gifford down there, no harm will be done". His brother [Henry] is with him, fortunately. It cannot, I think, be good for him to luxuriate in misery to this extent. He says he is going down for the sake of the girl he married, & who died more than twenty years ago. His family say *that* girl never existed, [i.e. Hardy's relatives were sceptical about Hardy's recollections of Emma] but she did exist to him [i.e. in his mind], no doubt.'
>
> 'The strange thing is that this goes on side by side with the reading of those diabolical diaries. I had hoped they were destroyed, but only the other night he produced one from his pocket & read me a passage - written about six weeks before her death - in which he says that her father & Mr *Putnam* were right in their estimate of TH's character: he is ... (... various oft' repeated adjectives of abuse ...) & "*utterly worthless*".'

George Haven Putnam: US publisher and author, who visited Max Gate with his wife Emily in June 1911.

> 'Of course Mr Putnam, if she means the publisher, could *never* have belittled Mr Hardy to her. It is in this sort of way that the diaries are so poisonous.'
>
> 'Fortunately TH. [Hardy] seems not to mind them so much now …. All I trust is that I may not, for the rest of his life, have to sit & listen humbly to an account of her virtues and graces.'
>
> 'It is very quiet & lonely here, but Mr H. returns on Monday, & I keep a loaded revolver in my bedroom.'[3]

Four days later, after she and Hardy had returned home to Max Gate, Florence described their visit to Cornwall: '[It] has been a very painful one to me, & I have said a dozen times I wish I had not come - What possessed me to do it!'[4] One may imagine Hardy at St Juliot, lost in thought for Emma and behaving as if Florence was not there!

Meanwhile, in early 1913, Hardy's brother Henry relocated from the Bockhampton family home to his own, purpose-built property, Talbothays Lodge, West Stafford, 2 miles distant. Designed by Hardy himself, the house was built on land that Henry had inherited from his father.[5] Here, he was joined by his sisters Mary and Kate from Dorchester, and by his cousin, Polly Antell.

On 18 January 1916, Florence, in a letter to Rebekah Owen, referred to 'the *awful* diary the first Mrs T. H. kept (which he burned) full of venom, hatred & abuse of him & his family'.[6]

On 6 September 1916 Hardy wrote to Reverend J. H. Dickinson to tell him that he and Florence planned to go to Tintagel 'this week for a couple of days, & also to Launceston [Cornwall] to see a relative of my late wife's'. He continued, 'My wife was a friend of the first Mrs Hardy and is naturally interested in seeing where she lived'. This was perhaps wishful thinking on Hardy's part![7]

On 15 June 1920 Hardy wrote to the Reverend J. H. Dickinson, describing Florence as 'having been a friend of Emma's', who had 'naturally been always interested in St Juliot & its associations'.[8] This again may represent a degree of wishful thinking by Hardy!

Evelyn Hardy said of Emma:

> 'From all that we can learn about her as a young woman she seems to have been impulsive, capable, courageous, and vital, possessing a certain childlike quality whereby she attracted and endeared herself to people, which never deserted her.[9] Florence, to her credit, confirmed this, when she told Vere Collins in 1920 that Emma 'kept to the end a strange lovableness – a gay,

inconsequent, childlike charm.'[10] In other words, despite Emma's increasingly antisocial behaviour, the fair-minded Florence did have *some* positive memories of her.

4. The Death of Hardy's Sister Mary

On 24 November 1915, three years after the death of Emma, Hardy's sister Mary died aged 73. This was an added grief for Hardy to bear. She was deeply lamented by him, and typically, he commemorated her in his poem *The Sun's Last Look on the Country Girl*.

Mary was buried in Stinsford churchyard. We 'buried her under the yew tree where the rest of us lie', wrote Hardy.[1]

5. Those who Beat a Path to Hardy's Door

It is unlikely that any other distinguished man or woman-of-letters of Hardy's era could boast of such a list of distinguished visitors that came to visit the great man at Max Gate. They included:

> Edward Clodd (writer); Clement Shorter (journalist and literary critic); Teresa Fetherstonhaugh (family friend and cousin of T. E. Lawrence); Sir Henry Hoare (landowner); Professor Flinders Petrie (Egyptologist); Mary Sheridan (of Frampton Court, Frampton, Dorset); Dorothy Allhusen (daughter of society hostess and organizer of charitable projects Mary Jeune, Lady St Helier); John Cowper Powys (philosopher, novelist, and critic); Siegfried Sassoon (poet, soldier, and writer); Charlotte Mew (poet); Harley Granville-Barker (actor, director, and critic) and his wife Helen; John Galsworthy (novelist and playwright); Robert Graves (poet, soldier, historical novelist, and critic); Margaret Soundy (Florence's sister) and her son Thomas; Sir James Barrie (Scottish novelist and playwright) and his secretary Lady Cynthia Asquith (writer and socialite); Edmund Blunden (poet, soldier, author, and critic); E. M. Forster (novelist); Ralph Bankes (Dorset landowner); H. G. Wells (writer and father of modern science fiction) and his mistress Rebecca West (author, journalist, critic, and travel writer); George Bernard Shaw (Irish playwright and political activist) and his wife Charlotte (Irish political activist); H. M. Tomlinson (writer and journalist) and his wife Florence; Hester, Lady Pinney, wife of Major-General Sir Reginald Pinney); Caroline Hanbury (Hardy's god-daughter); John

> Drinkwater (poet and dramatist); Philip Ridgeway (Director of the Barnes Theatre in south-west London); Virginia Woolf (modernist author) and her husband Leonard (political theorist, author, publisher, and civil servant); Middleton Murry (writer on religion, politics, and social issues); Henry Williamson (writer on wildlife, social issues, and ruralism); Sir Anthony Hope Hawkins (novelist and playwright); Augustine Birrell (Liberal Party politician); Sir Sidney Colvin (curator and literary art critic). But of all Hardy's visitors it was, arguably, T. E. Lawrence (archaeologist, soldier, diplomat, and writer), who used to roar up to the front door of Max Gate on his Brough Superior motorcycle, who he was most fond of.

Meanwhile, there followed the following poetry collections, reflecting Hardy's prodigious literary output: *Selected Poems* (1916); *Moments of Vision and Miscellaneous Verses* (1917); *Late Lyrics and Earlier with Many Other Verses* (1922); *The Famous Tragedy of the Queen of Cornwall* (poetic drama, 1923); *Human Shows, Far Phantasies, Songs and Trifles* (1925).

6. How Hardy Acknowledged the Fact of his Own Mortality

In his poem *Waiting Both* (published in 1925), Hardy compared himself to a star in the firmament. Each had a finite lifespan, and each was doomed to die:

> A star looks down at me,
> And says: 'Here I and you
> Stand, each in our degree:
>
> What do you mean to do, -
> Mean to do?'
>
> I say: 'For all I know,
> Wait, and let Time go by,
> Till my change come.' – 'Just so,'
> The star says: 'So mean I: -
> 'So mean I.'

7. Hardy's Incivility and Meanness

Does Hardy's relationship with the household staff at Max Gate shed any light on how he had behaved towards Emma? Hardy's gardener Bertie Stephens, who managed the one-acre garden, conservatory, greenhouse, and paddock single-handed, stated that 'At no time did Hardy express any appreciation or give any praise for anything that was done'. Hardy could also 'get into a bit a mood' and be 'irritable'.

Hardy's barber, W. G. Mills of Dorchester, stated that his client never gave a tip, or a Christmas present, but instead was always 'very close with his money'.

Hardy's cook Mrs A. Stanley described Hardy's trousers as being so worn that they had 'fringes' at their bottoms. 'He was too mean to buy himself a decent pair'. When, on Boxing Day, she gave the postman 2s 6d on behalf of the family, Hardy refused to reimburse her the money on the grounds that 'Dorchester people never give tips'.

Hardy's parlourmaid Miss Ellen E. Titterington stated that although Hardy gave the maids at Max Gate 'quiet little smiles as he passed them on the stairs, he never passed the time of day with them, unless it was to talk about the weather'. If she put too much coal on the fire, he would take it off again! Nevertheless, she was prepared to give him the benefit of the doubt. 'The memory of his early days when he was poor', she said, 'must have remained with him and influenced his behaviour'.

Hardy's cleaner Margaret Male stated that Hardy would never acknowledge people who worked for him if he passed them in the street. She attributed this to his shyness.

His chauffeur, Harold Voss, stated that he never saw Hardy in a temper. He was a 'real gentleman' who was 'never flurried' but always calm.

Paradoxically, in 1883, Hardy's article entitled 'The Dorsetshire Labourer', was published in *Longman's Magazine*. In it he indicated that his sympathies always lay with the poor and the oppressed. Such a person as the labourer, he said sympathetically, was hitherto personified as having an:

> 'uncouth manner and aspect, stolid understanding, and snail-like movement [who spoke with a] chaotic corruption of regular language, that few persons … consider it worth while to enquire what views, if any, of life, nature, or of Society, are conveyed in these utterances. He hangs his head and looks sheepish when spoken to and thinks Lunnon [London] is a place paved with gold. Misery and fever lurk in his cottage. He has few thoughts of joy, and little hope of rest.' In 1890, Hardy wrote:

> 'Altruism, or The Golden Rule, or whatever "Love your neighbour as Yourself" [the Second Commandment of Jesus in the *Holy Bible*'s New Testament Book of Matthew, 22:37-39] may be called, will ultimately be brought about I think by the pain we see in others reacting on ourselves, as if we and they were part

> of one body.'[1] Here, Hardy revealed himself to be, ostensibly, an extremely empathetic person.

Altruism: disinterested and selfless concern for the well-being of others.[2]

However, given Hardy's lack of consideration towards his household staff, it appears that his concern for 'ordinary folks' was of a purely theoretical nature!

Did Hardy's incivility extend to Emma, who came from a well-off middle-class family and who would therefore have been accustomed to a degree of luxury and decorum? Not initially, surely, when he was lovestruck by her beauty and charm. And in Emma's later years, they lived virtually separate lives. As for his parsimoniousness, the likelihood is that yes, the penny-pinching Hardy would not have gone out of his way to indulge his estranged wife, and this may have been another source of marital discord.[3]

As for Emma, she had a similar condescending attitude towards the 'lower orders' of society, but even so, according to Dolly Gale, she could be kind and considerate. Hardy's rudeness, however, disgusted Dolly and this was one reason why she despised him. But why *was* Hardy so uncivil? Did he consider himself superior to those who, by their labour, made it possible for Max Gate to function as a household? Or was it because he felt miserable living there? Perhaps it was a mixture of both.

The conclusion is that Hardy showed little civility to his staff, but to Voss his chauffeur, upon whom he depended, he was politeness itself!

8. Was Hardy a Pessimist?

Hardy has been criticized for being a dyed-in-the wool pessimist, defined as a tendency to see the worst aspect of things or believe that the worst will happen.[1] But this was not invariably the case. US professor, curator, and editor Carl J. Weber quoted Hardy as saying:

> 'I believe, indeed, that a good deal of the robustious, swaggering optimism of recent literature is at bottom cowardly and insincere. My pessimism, if pessimism it be, does not involve the assumption that the world is going to the dogs. On the contrary, my practical philosophy is distinctly meliorist.'

Meliorism: the belief that the world can be made better by human effort.[2]

'Whatever may be the inherent good or evil of life, it is certain that men make it much worse than it need be. When we have got rid of a thousand remediable ills, it will be time enough to determine whether the ill that is irremediable outweighs the good.'[3]

In other words, man had it in his power to undo the harm that he had done during his sojourn on earth.

'I confess I never saw Hardy laugh', said Flower, but there is no doubt that he enjoyed life at times:

> 'A happy smile would flick across his face like a flash of summer lightning. He would inwardly chuckle. He would relate a humorous happening he had known and rejoice in it. But I never saw him really laugh.'[4]

And in his later years, Hardy always looked forward with joyful anticipation, to hearing the church bells as they rang in the New Year. For example, on 31 December 1925, he wrote:

> 'F. [Florence] and I sat up. Heard on the wireless various features of New Year's Eve in London: dancing at the Albert Hall, Big Ben striking twelve, singing Auld Lang Syne, God save the King, Marseillaise, hurrahing.'[5]

From his home, Heytesbury House in Wiltshire on 20 September 1956, to Liberal politician Philip E. Morell, Sassoon wrote of Hardy:

> 'My own principal experience of him revealed him as a man who wanted to be cheerful – but his wistful philosophy is all there in his poems.'[6]

Wistful: having or showing a feeling of vague or regretful longing.[7]

9. Hardy and Persistent Complex Bereavement Disorder

Can Hardy's prolonged and profound adverse reaction to the death of his wife Emma be considered excessive, and does anyone have the right to judge it to be so? After all every relationship is different, and each person who loses a partner grieves in their own unique way. And, of course, no one ever asks, or deserves, to be placed in such a position. In Hardy's case, how could it be that he was so grief stricken and for so long, probably for the remainder of his days, given the couple's marital differences and their virtual estrangement in Emma's later years?

The death of a partner is traumatic enough in itself but paradoxically, when there are unresolved issues existing at the time when one of them dies, this can make the pain and heartache for the survivor even worse. After all there is now no opportunity for reconciliation, explanation, apology, contrition, etcetera. And what remains in the mind of the survivor is unutterable sadness and feelings of guilt and regret – 'If only!'. This was undoubtedly the case with Hardy.

Rightly or wrongly, the *Diagnostic and Statistical Manual of Mental Disorders* (Fifth Edition, published in 2013 by the American Psychiatric Association), describes the phenomenon of 'Persistent Complex Bereavement Disorder' (PCBD) which, by implication, is regarded as a significant mental disorder. For a diagnosis of PCBD to be made, the following criteria must be met. At least one year must have elapsed:

> 'since the death of someone with whom the bereaved had a close relationship. This time frame discriminates normal grief from persistent grief. The condition typically involves a persistent yearning/longing for the deceased, which may be associated with intense sorrow and frequent crying or preoccupation with the deceased.' Also, for the diagnosis to be confirmed, 'Six additional symptoms are required. They include:
>
> 'Marked difficulty accepting that the individual has died; disbelief that the individual is dead; distressing memories of the deceased; anger over the loss; maladaptive [i.e. negative] appraisals about oneself in relation to the deceased or the death; and excessive avoidance of reminders of the loss.' It will be remembered that Hardy reached a point where he found revisiting St Juliot too painful to contemplate.
>
> 'Individuals may also report a desire to die because they wish to be with the deceased; feel isolated; believe that life has no meaning or purpose without the deceased; experience a diminished sense of identity in which they feel a part of themselves has died or been lost.'

Finally, PCBD 'requires clinically significant distress or impairment in psychosocial functioning'.[1]

Psychosocial: the psychosocial approach looks at individuals in the context of the combined influence that psychological factors and the surrounding social environment have on their physical and mental wellness and their ability to function.[2]

Hardy displayed all of the above characteristics, to a greater or lesser degree.

10. How Hardy Cherished the Memory of Lost Loved Ones

In his poem *Friends Beyond* (published in 1898), Hardy reflected on friends from the Parish of Stinsford ('Mellstock') that he had known, and yet he could still imagine them talking to him. And in death, they had found peace at last.

WILLIAM Dewy, Tranter Reuben, Farmer Ledlow late
  at plough,
 Robert's kin, and John's, and Ned's,
And the Squire, and Lady Susan, lie in Mellstock
  churchyard now!
'Gone,' I call them, gone for good, that group of
  local hearts and heads;
 Yet at mothy curfew-tide,
And at midnight when the noon-heat breathes it
  back from walls and leads,
They've a way of whispering to me - fellow-wight
  who yet abide -
 In the muted, measured note
Of a ripple under archways, or a lone cave's
  Stillicide …

Hardy's poem *One We Knew* (published in 1909) was dedicated to the memory of his paternal grandmother Mary Hardy (1772-1857), who lived with the family at Higher Bockhampton for the first 16 years of Hardy's life:

I
She told how they used to form for the country
  dances —
 'The Triumph', 'The New-rigged Ship' —
To the light of the guttering wax in the panelled
  manses,
 And in cots to the blink of a dip.

II
She spoke of the wild 'poussetting' and
  'allemanding'
 On carpet, on oak, and on sod;
And the two long rows of ladies and gentlemen
  standing,
 And the figures the couples trod.

IV
She told of that far-back day when they learnt
astounded
Of the death of the King of France:
Of the Terror; and then of Bonaparte's unbounded
Ambition and arrogance.

VI
Of how his threats woke warlike preparations
Along the southern strand,
And how each night brought tremors and
trepidations
Lest morning should see him land.

VII
She said she had often heard the gibbet creaking
As it swayed in the lightning flash,
Had caught from the neighbouring town a small
child's shrieking
At the cart-tail under the lash.

VIII
With cap-framed face and long gaze into the embers
We seated around her knees —
She would dwell on such dead themes, not as one
who remembers,
But rather as one who sees.

Poussete: country dance.[1]
Allemandes: German dances.[2]

King of France: King Louis XVI who, on 21 January 1793 during the French Revolution, was condemned to death for high treason and crimes against the state and sent to the guillotine. His wife, Queen Marie-Antoinette suffered the same fate nine months later.

Terror: Reign of Terror unleashed by the Jacobins who seized control of the National Convention in June 1793.

Jacobins: the most radical and ruthless of the political groups formed in the wake of the French Revolution.

Bonaparte: Napoleon Bonaparte, French military and political leader who rose to prominence during the French Revolution (1789-1799).

Dear to Hardy was the sound of his late father's violin, which he commemorated in 1916 in the following eponymous poem *To My Father's Violin* (published in 1917), together with his wonderful harmonies, and how he used to play without the need of a musical score.

I
Does he want you down there
In the Nether Glooms where
The hours may be a dragging load upon him,
As he hears the axle grind
Round and round
Of the great world, in the blind
Still profound
Of the night-time? He might liven at the sound
Of your string, revealing you had not forgone him.

And Hardy is anxious to send a message, that his father will never be forgotten.

11. Hardy as a Subject for Psychological Study!

In respect of Emma's uncle, Archdeacon E. Hamilton Gifford, and of Emma's brother-in-law the Reverend Caddell Holder, said Florence, 'Mrs Hardy [Emma] was always so alive to the magnificence of these [i.e. such] connections'. As for Hardy himself, Florence declared, Hardy's 'extreme veneration for the Church is very puzzling, for neither of these clergyman was ever friendly to him …. The whole affair is a most curious psychological study'.[1]

Chapter 20

Further Likely Reasons for Emma's Dislike of Hardy

Emma disapproved of Hardy for several reasons. He lacked a Christian faith; he had a propensity to flirt with other women (if not to be actually unfaithful to Emma - and there is evidence that he was, as already mentioned), a fact of which she was undoubtedly aware; he was miserly and parsimoniousness, which probably would not have impressed her, especially when he became wealthy and famous. But this was not all.

In a letter from Emma to Elspeth Grahame (née Thomson), wife of Scottish writer Kenneth Grahame, Emma revealed more of her innermost feelings towards her husband. In summer 1899, Elspeth wrote to Emma for advice on her marriage, which had taken place on 12 May of that year, and which was not going well. Emma replied cautiously, first enquiring:

> 'Do I know your choice [i.e. Grahame], perhaps I have met him, perhaps not. However, it is impossible to give "directions for use" — besides characters change so greatly with time, and circumstances. I can scarcely think that love proper and enduring is in the nature of men — as a rule — perhaps there is no woman "whom custom will not stale".'

This quotation derives from William Shakespeare's play *Antony and Cleopatra*: 'Age Cannot Wither Her, Nor Custom Stale Her Infinite Variety', and it indicates that Emma was well read! She continued:

> 'There is ever a desire to give but little in return for our devotion, & affection — theirs being akin to children's - a sort of easy affectionate*ness* - & at fifty, a man's feelings too often take a new course altogether. Eastern ideas of matrimony secretly pervade his thoughts, & he wearies of the most perfect & suitable wife chosen in his earlier life. Of course, he gets over it usually somehow, or hides it, or is lucky!' Emma advised Elspeth as follows:

> 'Keeping separate a good deal is a wise plan in crises - and being both free — and expecting little [,] neither gratitude, nor attention, love, nor *justice*, nor anything you may set your heart on - Love interest - adoration, & all that kind of thing is usually a failure complete — some one comes by [Emma presumably had in mind another female to whom Hardy was attracted] & upsets your pail of milk in the end — If he belongs to the public in any way [i.e. becomes famous, like Hardy], years of devotion count for nothing — Influence can seldom be retained as years go by, & *hundreds* of wives go through a phase of disillusion - it is really a pity to have any ideals in the first place.'[1]

When these statements are compared with Emma's account, in her *Recollections*, of those blissful early days with Hardy at St Juliot, they reveal an incredibly sad state of affairs. Emma feels that her husband is undemonstrative; she no longer expects anything from him; she believes that his adoring public is more important to him than she is; and she concludes that it is preferable, in the main, to keep out of the way and live separately from him, viz. her taking up residence in Max Gate's attic rooms.

Hardy had a lifelong fascination with corpses, as Emma found when, on their visit to Paris in autumn 1874, he took her with him on a visit to the city's mortuary – 'La Morgue'. Her reaction? 'Three bodies – middle one pink – Their clothes hanging above them. Not offensive but repulsive'.[2]

Chapter 21

Did Emma *Ever* Love Hardy?

The answer to this question is a resounding yes! After Emma's death, Hardy discovered:

> 'among her effects … a small volume bound in brown paper, stitched together with red string and written on lined leaves of exercise-book paper. It was headed "Some Recollections by E. L. Hardy", and its 70-odd pages ran to about 15,000 words. Its final page was dated 4 January 1911, and from internal signs it seems to have been written in the second half of the previous year. It is an autobiography of Emma's childhood, youth, and early womanhood, up to the time of their marriage.'[1]

In contrast to what Florence described as Emma's 'diabolical diaries', in which she heaped abuse on Hardy, Emma, in *Some Recollections*, stated that when she met Hardy, her:

> 'life's romance now began. Scarcely any author and his wife could have had a much more romantic meeting with its unusual circumstances, in bringing them together from two different though neighbouring counties to this one at this very remote spot, with beautiful sea-coast, and the wild Atlantic ocean rolling in with its magnificent waves and spray, its white gulls and black choughs and grey puffins, its cliffs and rocks and gorgeous sunsettings sparkling redness in a track widening from the horizon to the shore.'[2]

So, just as Hardy looked back to idyllic times spent with Emma during their courting days, so Emma looked back to that time as encompassing the great romantic period of her life. And given the fact that the couple were able to meet only infrequently during those times, how precious those occasions must have seemed!

When Hardy arrived at St Julitta's Rectory, said Emma:

> 'I was immediately arrested by his familiar appearance, as if I had seen him in a dream — his slightly different accent, his soft voice .... After this our first meeting, there had to be many visits to the Church, and these visits of deep interest for both, merged in those of acquaintance and affection to end in marriage, but not until after four years. [However] At first, though I was greatly interested in him, the Church matters were paramount.'[3] Subsequently, said Emma, Hardy:

> 'came two or three times a year from that time to visit me. I rode my pretty mare Fanny and he walked by my side and I showed him some of the neighbourhood — the cliffs, along the roads, and through the scattered hamlets, sometimes gazing down at the solemn small shores where the seals lived, coming out of great caverns very occasionally. We sketched and talked of books; often we walked down the beautiful Valley to Boscastle harbour where we had to jump over stones and climb over a low wall by rough steps, get through by narrow pathways to come out on great wide spaces suddenly, with a sparkling little brook going the same way, into which we once lost a tiny picnic-tumbler, and there it is to this day no doubt between two small boulders.' In fact, Hardy made a sketch of Emma as she attempted to retrieve it.
>
> 'Sometimes we all drove to Tintagel and [nearby] Trebarwith Strand where donkeys were onerously employed to get seaweed for the farmers; Strangles Beach [between Tintagel and Bude] also, Bossiney [hamlet on the outskirts of Tintagel], other places on the coast. Lovely drives they were, with sea views all along at intervals, and very dawdling enjoyable slow ones; sometimes to visit a neighbouring clergyman and his family.'
>
> 'We grew much interested in each other. I found him a perfectly new subject of study and delight, and he found a "mine" [presumably a gold mine!] in me, he said; he was quite unlike any other person who came to see us, for they were slow of speech and ideas!'

Can anyone doubt that this was true love?

> 'In the intervals of his visits we corresponded, and I studied and sketched and drove my brother-in-law and my sister in the basket-carriage to the nearest market town Camelford nine miles off, or to Launceston to see my cousins.'[4]

'After a little time, I copied a good deal of manuscript [Hardy's novel *Desperate Remedies*] which went to-and-fro by post, and I was very proud and happy doing this, which I did in the privacy of my room, where I read and wrote also the *letters*. The rarity of the visits made them highly delightful to both; we talked much of plots, possible scenes, tales, and poetry and of his own work.'

Here, Emma revealed that she was deeply involved with Hardy in his literary endeavours.

'He came either from Dorset or London, driving to and from Launceston [Train] Station, eighteen miles off. The day we were married was a perfect September day — 17th, 1874 — not a brilliant sunshine, but wearing a soft, sunny luminousness; just as it should be.'

'I have had various experiences, interesting some, sad others, since that lovely day, but all showing that an Unseen Power of great benevolence directs my ways; I have some philosophy and mysticism, and an ardent belief in Christianity and the life beyond this present one, all which makes any existence curiously interesting. As one watches *happenings* (and even if should occur *unhappy happenings*) outward circumstances are of less importance if Christ is our highest ideal. A strange unearthly brilliance shines around our path, penetrating and dispersing difficulties with its warmth and glow.'[5]

Emma evidently composed *Some Recollections* between summer 1910, when she had been married to Hardy for 35 years, and January 1911, just under 2 years before her death. What is surprising is that despite the unhappy state of her marriage, she was able to rejoice in the memory of her courting days four decades previously and record her memories of it without any rancour or bitterness. It is also remarkable that her Christian faith sustained her, despite all her unhappy earthly experiences.

Chapter 22

How Did Hardy Survive the Loss of Emma? His Coping Mechanisms

To lose a beloved partner is a terrible enough experience to have to bear. But the presence of unresolved or unresolvable issues between the partners prior to the bereavement, as was certainly the case with Hardy and Emma, made such an experience even more unbearable for the survivor. For now, there was no possibility of reconciliation, or of rekindling the profound and unconditional love that had once existed between the two of them. And the final straw for Hardy was when he discovered, after her death, that Emma had written two books, criticizing him in the most vehement manner.

1. How the Mind Deals with Memories

When a person is in deep grief, it is difficult or impossible for him or her to imagine that such grief will ever fade, that it will ever be possible to live anything approaching a normal life again; or even that it will be possible to carry on living. However, in the modern world, grief councillors give an assurance that the grief will dull, even if it never goes away entirely.

Said Kübler-Ross and Kessler:

> 'When you sit with the dying and their family, the loved ones will often say that part of them is dying too. That is true, but equally true is that a part of the one who died lives on in us. At a recent memorial service, the minister told the congregation, "You have not lost all of the things that you loved most about your loved one. They are in you. You carry them with you for the rest of your life".'[1]
>
> 'A year ago, or years ago, you were a different person. The person you were is forever changed. A part of the old you died with your loved one. And a part of your loved one lives on in the new you.'[2]

The authors clearly saw the retaining of the memory of the loved one as something positive, and doubtless countless others see it in a similar light. For many however, it is a bitter/sweet phenomenon, in that recalling those happy memories of joys once shared may be a source of pain and anguish over what is now lost forever. But the passage of time may play a part in that in time, the heartache fades.

In Hardy's case, there is no doubt from his poems and writings that Emma's memory stayed with him for the remainder of his days.

Experience shows that yes, our mindset does change after a prolonged period of grief, but how does this come about?

Despite advances in neuroscience, human memory and human emotion at a molecular level are little understood, and in the meantime, it is necessary to construct a hypothetical model to try to understand these two phenomena.

Human experience suggests that the brain compartmentalizes information, in order that it can easily be recalled. Suppose that the compartments are located in a circle around the brain, all at an equal radius from the centre, and the length of the radius represents the ease and accuracy with which each memory can be recalled. But given the fact that distant memories tend to fade, this cannot be a true representation. Alternatively, suppose that the 'memory compartments' are arranged vertically like a stack of bricks, the most recent one being nearest to the brain and the most distant one the furthest away. And again, suppose that the distance from brain to compartment represents the ease and accuracy with which each memory can be recalled.

So, following a bereavement, as new memories are laid down and compartmentalized, so the compartmentalized 'bereavement memory' will recede. This is perhaps why a person who had lost his or her partner but has the company and support of friends and family, varied interests, and is independently mobile, is more likely to recover faster than someone who is alone and housebound. This is because, for the former, a wealth of new memories will serve to put the 'bereavement memory' in perspective.

This said, however, one size does not fit all and for those with good recall, memory of their bereavement, with all the attendant horrors of flashbacks, may remain forever fresh and painful in their minds. This definitely appears to have been the case with Hardy, vis-à-vis Emma!

2. How Distractions Offered Hardy a Diversion from Painful Memories

To Lady Ilchester on 21 January 1913 Hardy described how, after Emma's death, 'the monotonous duties of life insist on being attended to, & so the mind gets diverted from broodings.'[1]

Another distraction for Hardy was to pay visits to his numerous friends and acquaintances. For example:

> Sir James Barrie (London); Sir Walter and Lady Raleigh (Oxford); Mary, Henry, and Kate Hardy at Talbothays (West Stafford, Dorset); Florence Henniker (Southwold, Suffolk); Edward Clodd (Aldeburgh, Suffolk); Sydney Cockerell (Cambridge); Sir Sidney Colvin (London); John Lane (Blandford Forum, Dorset); Stuart Alexander Donaldson (Master of Magdalene College, Cambridge and Vice-Chancellor of the University); Lady St Helier (London); Sir Henry and Lady Hoare (Stourhead, Wiltshire); Sir Frederick and Lady Treves (Richmond, south-west London); Lady Ilchester (Melbury House, Melbury Osmond, Dorset).

Hardy also went motoring with Florence and Kate, and walking, and cycling, and was chauffeured all over Dorset and beyond by Harold Voss, or by author, photographer, and animal lover Hermann Lea. He also went on cycling expeditions with Florence; attended rehearsals and performances of dramatizations of his novels by the Hardy Players at the Corn Exchange, Dorchester; engaged in voluminous correspondence; officiated as a Justice of the Peace; visited Aberdeen, Oxford, Cambridge, St Andrew's, and Bristol, to receive the honorary degrees which the universities of those cities had conferred upon him. And, of course, he continued to write his wonderful poetry.

The influence on Hardy of having the companionship of Florence's fox terrier 'Wessex' cannot be overestimated. 'Wessex' was born in August 1913, 9 months after Emma's death, and not long afterwards became an integral and colourful part of the Hardy household. Despite 'Wessex's' bad behaviour, Hardy became his devoted admirer. For his master, the terrier could do no wrong, even to the extent of being permitted to roam the tabletop at mealtimes in search of tit bits, either freely given or stolen from the plates of whoever happened to by dining at the time, and irrespective of the status of the guests! Anyone who has been bereaved will attest to the comfort that a pet dog or cat may bring, especially if he of she finds themselves alone in an empty house and there is no doubt, from Hardy's description of 'Wessex', that the dog helped to keep him sane and grounded during this utterly traumatic time of his life.

3. Revisiting Former Haunts

In his poem *After a Journey* (published in 1914), Hardy revealed that he was inexorably drawn to revisit the scenes of his courtship of Emma. He also implied that in his endless search for Emma, it was she who was instrumental in leading him to their former haunts. In the poem, Hardy also implied that although their relationship had begun well, it had ended in division.

II
Yes: I have re-entered your olden haunts at last;
   Through the years, through the dead scenes I have tracked you;
What have you now found to say of our past -
   Scanned across the dark space wherein I have lacked you?
Summer gave us sweets, but autumn wrought division?
      Things were not lastly as firstly well
         With us twain, you tell?
But all's closed now, despite Time's derision.

III
I see what you are doing: you are leading me on
   To the spots we knew when we haunted here together,
The waterfall, above which the mist-bow shone
   At the then fair hour in the then fair weather,
And the cave just under, with a voice still so hollow
   That it seems to call out to me from forty years ago,
      When you were all aglow,
And not the thin ghost that I now frailly follow!

The poem ends:

IV
Trust me, I mind not, though Life lours,
      The bringing me here; nay, bring me here again!
         I am just the same as when
Our days were a joy, and our paths through flowers.

In other words, for Hardy, the revisiting of his and Emma's favourite haunts was a kind of therapy for him, a way of coping with the greatest trauma of his life, a mode of survival. However, this was not always the case and sometimes he found that such visits made him sad.

4. How Hardy Came to Depend on Florence: Mutual Support

After the death of Emma, said Flower, Hardy:

'was alone in the house now, save for the servants. His dead wife lay in her room and this state of Tragedy numbed his mind. He telegraphed to his late wife's friend, Florence Dugdale, who had so often stayed at the house. She was never his secretary as has been so often stated. During her visits to Max Gate she had done no more than put his papers in order before she departed again. She came now in response to his telegram.'[1]

In other words, Florence was a support to Hardy, right from the start of his bereavement.

In a letter to Florence dated 29 January 1913, Hardy wrote:

'If I once get you here again won't I clutch you tight: you shall stay till spring. I felt very sad & lonely yesterday: not quite so much today.'[2]

To Florence Henniker on 17 July 1914, Hardy wrote to say:

'We are going on calmly enough here as you guess. She [Florence] is a very tender companion & is quite satisfied with the quietude of life here.'[3]

To Alda, Lady Hoare on 9 December 1914, Florence wrote of Hardy:

'I do know he has a tender protective affection for me - as a father for a child - as he has always had - a feeling quite apart from passion. And I feel towards him, sometimes, as a mother towards a child with whom things have somehow gone wrong - a child who needs comforting - to be treated gently & with all the love possible.'[4]

5. Hardy's Memorial to Emma

It was doubtless a comfort to Hardy to organize the placing of the aforementioned memorial tablet to Emma in the church at St Juliot, and on 1 June 1913 he wrote as follows to the Reverend J. H. Dickinson in this regard:

'I learn from Mr Geach the monumental mason that he has placed the tablet in St Juliot [St Julitta's] Church, & that it has a very good appearance. Also, that you are satisfied with it. I am very glad that this is the case.'

> 'It was a pleasure for me to be able to inscribe upon it that my late wife laid the foundation stone for the rebuilding - a fact that I had forgotten till reminded by a note in an old diary of hers. I can now recall that Mr [the Reverend Caddell] Holder gave the schoolchildren a tea on the occasion, & made a speech to them asking them to remember the event. I should very much like to see the memorial, but sad memories so crowded upon me when I last visited the spot that I suppose I shall never venture to go again.'[1]

Hardy evidently, no longer found solace in revisiting the scenes of his former courting days with Emma. But he subsequently changed his mind. To novelist and playwright John Galsworthy on 16 April 1916, Hardy wrote regarding himself and Florence:

> 'We both want to go West … to see if a tablet to my first wife, who was also a great friend of my present wife's, has been put up properly in St Juliot Church, near Boscastle.'[2]

On 4 September 1916 Hardy wrote to Florence Henniker to inform her that he and Florence planned to visit Cornwall:

> 'for 3 or 4 days this week, starting I believe Thursday. The memories it will revive will of course be rather sad ones for me, but I want to see the tablet that has been erected in St Juliot Church, near Boscastle, to Emma, recording that she lived there, played [the harmonium[3]] in church, laid the foundation stone of the new part, &c. & Florence wants to see the place & the cliff scenery, never having been there.'

As a reminder that the First World War was still in progress, Hardy continued:

> 'The morning papers have this moment arrived, telling us that a Zeppelin [enemy airship] was brought down near London on Saturday.'[4]

6. A Continuity of Lifestyle

Hardy was a creature of habit, who disliked any disruption to his normal routine. Florence was therefore the ideal companion, as will be seen.

On 16 February 1914, Hardy wrote to the Reverend J. H. Dickinson thanking him (and his wife) 'for his good wishes on my marriage':

> 'The step has been soberly taken, I may even say gravely, that my wife & I hope we shall not be disappointed in it.' Nevertheless, Hardy continued, 'The romance of S. [St] Juliot abides, & will if I live to be a hundred. Indeed, one of the satisfactions of my present position is that my wife was a great friend of my late wife, so that there is no rupture of continuity in my life, which always seems an added sadness in a world that at the best is so transitory & full of severances.'[1]

To essayist and academic A. C. Benson on 2 March 1914, Hardy wrote in similar vein:

> 'I have known my wife many years, & she was a friend of my first wife as she has been for a long time of my sisters, so that that there is not that rupture of continuity in my life by this event [i.e. his marriage to Florence] which I so much dislike.'[2]

On 17 September 1914 Hardy wrote to jurist and historian Frederic Harrison to say, in respect of his marriage to Florence:

> 'That the union of two rather melancholy temperaments may result in cheerfulness, as the junction of two negatives forms a positive, is our modest hope. It may seem odd to you, but the sense of continuity through her having been attached to my late wife is not the least part of my satisfaction.'[3]

In other words, Florence, because of her magnanimous, friendly, and forgiving attitude towards Emma, had given Hardy more peace of mind than would otherwise have been the case.

But all was not sweetness and light. In his poem *Nobody Comes* (composed on 9 October 1924 and published in 1925), Hardy implied that even when he had married Florence and they were living together at Max Gate, he was lonely and, by implication, still missing Emma dreadfully:

> II
> A car comes up, with lamps full-glare,
> That flash upon a tree:
> It has nothing to do with me,
> And whangs along in a world of its own,
> Leaving a blacker air;
> And mute by the gate I stand again alone,
> And nobody pulls up there.

7. Did Hardy Find Any Solace in Religion?

Florence recorded that on 26 April 1882, Hardy attended the funeral of naturalist, biologist, and geologist Charles Darwin (1809-1882) in Westminster Abbey. Darwin was co-author, with naturalist and explorer Alfred Russel Wallace, of the theory of evolution.

Said Florence, Hardy 'as a young man' was 'among the earliest acclaimers of *The Origin of Species*'. This followed the publication on 24 November 1859 of Darwin's book *On the Origin of Species by Means of Natural Selection.*

Darwin stated that man (and all other animals) had evolved, rather than created as stated in the *Holy Bible*'s Book of Genesis. This was reflected by Hardy in his poem *Drinking Song* (published in 1928):

> Next this strange message Darwin brings,
> (Though saying his say
> In a quiet way);
> We all are one with creeping things;
> And apes and men
> Blood-brethren,
> And likewise reptile forms with stings.

Darwin also indicated that evolution had occurred over a vastly longer timescale than that is envisaged in the *Bible*. And given that the story of creation was just that, a story, Hardy must have wondered if any of the other accounts contained in the *Bible* were true. The experience of learning about Darwin's Theory of Evolution was probably the catalyst which first sowed doubt in Hardy's mind and led him to become an atheist.

In a further volume, *The Descent of Man and Selection in Relation to Sex* (published in 1871), Darwin went as far as to say that 'man is descended from a hairy, tailed quadruped, probably arboreal in its habits'. Nowadays, of course, it is generally accepted that man and the apes evolved from a common ancestor. (Curiously enough, neither of the above volumes were to be found in Hardy's personal library, extensive though it was.)

> 'Evidence from fossils, proteins and genetic studies indicates that humans and chimpanzees had a common ancestor millions of years ago. Most scientists believe that the 'human' family tree (known as the sub-group hominin) split from the chimpanzees and other apes about five to seven million years ago.'[1]

Hardy's poem *A Plaint to Man* was composed in 1909-1910 and published in 1914. In it, following the death of Emma in November 1912, he could now give full vent to his feelings on the subject of religion, which he declared to be simply an invention of mankind.

In the poem, the roles of God and man are reversed, the message of the poem, as writer and retired librarian John Welford declared, being 'God is a human construct'... and 'Man has created God in his own image'. Furthermore, 'God's advice to Man is to welcome this event' – i.e., the knowledge that God does not actually exist, and 'to throw away the crutch of manmade religion'. Man must 'ensure' that this "fact must be faced", and it would have been far better if it had been "faced in earlier years"'.

I
When you slowly emerged from the den of Time,
And gained percipience as you grew,
And fleshed you fair out of shapeless slime,

II
Wherefore, O Man, did there come to you
The unhappy need of creating me -
A form like your own - for praying to?

III
My virtue, power, utility,
Within my maker must all abide,
Since none in myself can ever be.

In other words, it is *man* who possesses these qualities, *and not God, who man invented*!

V
"Such a forced device", you may say, "is meet
For casing a loaded heart at whiles:
Man needs to conceive of a mercy-seat

VI
Somewhere above the gloomy aisles
Of this wailful world, or he could not bear
The irk no local hope beguiles".

In other words, had God not been invented, people would have found certain aspects of human life to be unbearable: for example, in Hardy's case, the death of Emma.

VIII
And now that I dwindle day by day
Beneath the deicide eyes of seers
In a light that will not let me stay,

Deicide: the killer of a god.[2]

In other words, those who are wise and knowledgeable have realized the truth of the matter – that God is an invention.

IX
And to-morrow the whole of me disappears,
The truth should be told, and the fact be faced
That had best been faced in earlier years:

X
The fact of life with dependence placed
On the human heart's resource alone,
In brotherhood bonded close and graced

XII
With loving-kindness fully blown,
And visioned help unsought, unknown.

Plaint: accusation of charge.[3]

Percipience: having a good understanding of things.[4]

Vivify: enliven.[5]

Meet: suitable or proper.[6]

Case: protective covering.[7]

At whiles: at times.[8]

Mercy-seat: the throne of God regarded as a place of divine access, communion, or propitiation.[9]

Irk: irritate, annoy.[10]

Seer: a person of supposed supernatural insight who sees visions of the future.[11]

In other words, said Welford, the poem is saying that:

> 'Since there is nothing outside mankind in spiritual terms, as shown by the fact that God is an invention of Man, the best course of action is to look inwards rather than outwards ("dependence placed/On the human heart's resource alone") and for men and women to rely on each other for support when times get tough ("In brotherhood bonded close").'[12]

In his song entitled *Saying Good-bye* (published in 1922), Hardy remembered those who had died during his lifetime, but as far as he was concerned, they were now simply deceased, and he expected never to hear from them again. Furthermore, there was no mention of an afterlife, resurrection from the dead, or heaven, only mention of the tomb; (burial) mound; clay (into which the body is transformed after death); worms eating away at the flesh; phantoms; ghosts. This, of course, is in accordance with his views as an atheist:

I
We are always saying
    'Good-bye, good-bye!'
In work, in playing,
In gloom, in gaying:
    At many a stage
    Of pilgrimage
    From youth to age
    We say, 'Good-bye,
        Good-bye!'

II
We are undiscerning
    Which go to sigh,
Which will be yearning
For soon returning;
    And which no more
    Will dark our door,
    Or tread our shore,
    But go to die,
        To die.

IV
So, with this saying,
    'Good-bye, good-bye,'
We speed their waying

Without betraying
    Our grief, our fear
    No more to hear
    From them, close, clear,
    Again: 'Good-bye,
        Good-bye!'

Those who have lost a beloved partner will immediately identify with the words, 'grief', and 'fear', which invariably follow such loss.

For Hardy, there was no solace to be found in religion, even when members of his family died, as his poem *The Sun's Last Look on the Country Girl (M.H)*, composed in December 1915 following the death of his sister Mary (and published in 1922) indicates. Much as they had loved each other in life, there was *no possibility* that they would be reunited in death:

The sun threw down a radiant spot
    On the face in the winding-sheet —
The face it had lit when a babe's in its cot;
And the sun knew not, and the face knew not
    That soon they would no more meet.

Now that the grave has shut its door,
    And lets not in one ray,
Do they wonder that they meet no more —
That face and its beaming visitor —
    That met so many a day?

Chapter 23

How Scientific Advances Have Shed a Different Light on the Authenticity of Religion

In his poem *A Cathedral Façade at Midnight* (published in 1925), Hardy made it clear that, as far as religion was concerned, reason had now replaced the ancient 'creeds':

III
A frail moan from the martyred saints there set
    Mid others of the erection
Against the breeze, seemed sighings of regret
    At the ancient faith's rejection
Under the sure, unhasting, steady stress
Of Reason's movement, making meaningless
The coded creeds of old-time godliness.

Erection: presumably figures carved in stone on the cathedral façade.

Chapter 24

How Hardy Mourned his Loss of Faith

In his poem *The Impercipient* (published in 1898), Hardy, having attended a cathedral service, poignantly expressed regret at his lack of Christian faith:

> 'O doth a bird deprived of wings
> Go earth—bound wilfully?'

In his poem *God's Funeral* (published in 1914), said Evelyn Hardy, Hardy 'mourns the loss of faith' (including, no doubt, his own) which had 'upheld those who have lived in former ages':[1]

> XI
> How sweet it was in years far hied
> To start the wheels of day with trustful prayer,
> To lie down liegely at the eventide
> And feel a blest assurance he [God] was there!
>
> XII
> And who or what shall fill his place?
> Whither will wanderers turn distracted eyes
> For some fixed star to stimulate their pace
> Towards thc goal of their enterprise?' …
>
> XIII
> Some in the background then I saw,
> Sweet women, youths, men, all incredulous,
> Who chimed as one: 'This is a counterfeit of straw,
> This requiem mockery! Still he lives to us!'
>
> XIV
> I could not prop their faith: and yet
> Many I had known: with all I sympathized;

And though struck speechless, I did not forget
That what was mourned for, I, too, once had prized.

XV
Still, how to bear such loss I deemed
The insistent question for each animate mind,
And gazing, to my growing sight there seemed
A pale yet positive gleam low down behind,

XVI
Whereof, to lift the general night,
A certain few who stood aloof had said,
"See you upon the horizon that small light -
Swelling somewhat?" Each mourner shook his head.

XVII
And they composed a crowd of whom
Some were right good, and many nigh the best …
Thus dazed and puzzled 'twixt the gleam and gloom
Mechanically I followed with the rest.

Hie: to go quickly.[2]

Liege: concerned with or relating to the relationship between a feudal superior and a vassal.[3]

Vassal: a holder of land by feudal tenure on conditions of homage and allegiance.[4]

Prop: support.[5]

Of 'God's Funeral', John Welford declared:

> 'The narrator decides to follow the procession and he is thus able to overhear the comments of some of the mourners. They lament that they are no longer able to keep alive their creation on which they have come to depend. They describe how they changed their conception of God down the years, beginning with the Old Testament deity who [and he quoted from the poem], was "jealous, fierce" and later [presumably in the New Testament] assigning to him the qualities of justice, willingness to bless, and the supplier of "mercies manifold".'

> 'However, they then went too far ("tricked by our own early dream/And need of solace") and "grew self-deceived", so that "what we had imagined we believed". As a result, they "Mangled the Monarch of our fashioning" who "now has ceased to be".'
>
> 'They lament the loss of their comfort blanket and wonder what can take God's place. Hardy expresses this neatly as a desire for another Bethlehem birth.'
>
> 'Some of the mourners refuse to belief that God is actually dead, saying "Still he lives to us!" Hardy's response is that he can give them no comfort, but he also admits that he was once of their number: "I did not forget/That what was mourned for, I, too, long had prized".'
>
> 'He takes the view that everyone must answer the question of what to put in God's place in their own way, and that there is no catch-all solution. However, he also says that he can see "a pale yet positive gleam low down behind". Some of those present ("a certain few who stood aloof") agree that they can see, on the horizon, a "small light/Swelling somewhat", but most of the mourners shake their heads.'
>
> 'The final stanza declares that the people present contain some who are "right good, and many nigh the best". Clearly there is no consensus about the future course, and Hardy admits to being "dazed and puzzled 'twixt the gleam and gloom". He sees no option but to follow the procession with the rest.'
>
> 'Hardy does not indicate what the "gleam" might be, which is probably why it is a good idea to read *God's Funeral* alongside *A Plaint to Man*, because that poem does furnish a few clues. Basically, Hardy sees the solution for a world without a personal God as lying within the individual and with people working together in brotherhood.'[6]

In 1920, Hardy described himself as 'churchy – not in an intellectual sense, but in so far as instincts and emotions ruled'.[7] In other words, he reluctantly admitted that his head ruled his heart.

Chapter 25

Proof of Hardy's Recovery, Albeit Fragile!

On a happier note, Florence was able to report to Clodd, on 7 March 1913, that Hardy:

> 'has been extremely well in health, & quite cheerful. Fortunately, I have no anxiety concerning TH's health - he seems more vigorous & well than I have known him for some years.'[1]

To Clodd on 20 April 1913, Florence wrote of Hardy:

> 'You will be glad to know that he seems in most excellent spirits, & has said to me once or twice, with the zest of a schoolboy, "I *do* feel I like the idea of going to see Clodd at Aldeburgh [Suffolk]. I am quite up to it – now".'[2]

On 21 August 1913 Florence wrote to Clodd as follows:

> 'TH, I am glad to say, is in good health, & wonderfully cheerful. He has had no fit of depression for quite a long time.' And in a postscript, she added:

> 'Really he is wonderfully well & in unusually high spirits, Mr John Lane [publisher], who came down a week or two ago & paid a flying visit said he had not seen him look so well & so bright, for years.'[3]

Chapter 26

The Death of Hardy (11 January 1928)

Hardy died at his home at Max Gate on 11 January 1928. In his poem *'I Look into My Glass'* (published in 1898), he had indicated that he could have faced the prospect of death with equanimity, had it not been for the fact that his 'heart' – i.e. his emotions, were still involved with those who had gone before. In other words, he was concerned, not about his own death, but with the fact that with his death, the memories of those who were dear to him would also be lost:

I look into my glass,
And view my wasting skin,
And say, 'Would God it came to pass
My heart had shrunk as thin!'

For then, I, undistrest
By hearts grown cold to me,
Could lonely wait my endless rest
With equanimity.

But Time, to make me grieve,
Part steals, lets part abide;
And shakes this fragile frame at eve
With throbbings of noontide.

Hardy's wish had been to have a modest burial in his home county of Dorset. However, because of his fame, his friends campaigned for him to be buried in Poets' Corner, Westminster Abbey. This was thought to be appropriate because, as Hardy had once told Flower, he always thought of himself first and foremost as a poet:

> 'I gave up writing novels because I was tired of that form of expression. The only novel I wrote for which I have deep

> affection was *Jude the Obscure*. Years and years ago [poet and literary critic] Coventry Patmore told me that my proper form of expression was verse. I did not believe him. I told him that I thought he was utterly wrong. One day … one day sitting in my room I realized that he was right. The certainty of it came upon me suddenly. My novels mean nothing to me any more. They are pieces of my life, like Youth and the Middle-aged years that have passed away as stale. If I am remembered for anything — and I don't suppose that will happen to me — it will be for my verse.'[1]
> Hardy, in his modesty, could not have been more wrong!

A compromise was reached and on 16 January 1928 Hardy's ashes were interred in Westminster Abbey, while his heart was simultaneously buried in the same tomb as Emma at Stinsford in Dorset.

Even in death, Hardy was not able to escape the censure of the church, when the Dean of Westminster, the Very Reverend Dr William Foxley Norris received complaints:

> 'about a non-Christian being buried in such a prominent Christian site. On the day of the funeral, the Dean wrote to Hardy's local vicar to ask for reassurances that Hardy was indeed a Christian.'[2]

Chapter 27

Science Sheds New Light on 'Complicated Grief'

In January 2018, in an article entitled 'How to Help Someone with Complicated Bereavement: Fostering Understanding and Seeking Treatment', Elisabeth Kvarnstrom explained why some people suffer from complicated grief, but the majority do not.

Kvarnstrom stated that 'When someone you love can't get past their grief, you may feel helpless, confused, and frustrated'. This is surely how Hardy wife Florence must have felt in respect of her husband Hardy, after the death of Emma!

According to the US Diagnostic and Statistical Manual of Mental Disorders, some 7-10 per cent of people who experience bereavement subsequently suffer from 'Chronic Bereavement Syndrome', or 'Complicated Grief' (CG) as it is now commonly known. This is characterized by intense yearning for and preoccupation with the deceased, persisting for more than 12 months. Was Hardy such a sufferer? Undoubtedly, yes. For example, for almost a decade after Emma's death in 1912, he wrote numerous agonized poems in her memory. Today, over a century later, studies of the brain have shed new light on the matter.

'In 2008', said Kvarnstrom, 'researchers at UCLA used brain imaging technology to investigate differences in brain activity between people with complicated bereavement and those with healthy experiences of grief. The study showed that for those with complicated bereavement, reminders of their loved one activates neural reward activity in the brain'. Kvarnstrom quoted US Professor of Psychiatry Mary-Frances O'Connor, lead author of the study, as follows: 'The idea is that when our loved ones are alive, we get a rewarding cue from seeing them or things that remind us of them. After the loved one dies, those who adapt to the loss stop getting this neural reward. But those who don't adapt continue to crave it, because each time they do see a cue, they still get that neural reward'.

Whether Hardy continually looked at photographs of his late wife Emma, and at her portrait, is not known. However, from the poems that he wrote, eulogizing her after her death and bewailing his fate at losing her, it is clear that he was constantly reliving in his mind their early times together, beginning with when he first met her at St Juliot. So, how does this 'Neural Reward System' operate? In September 2023, in an article entitled 'Brain Reward System', Olivia Guy-Evans stated as follows:

> 'The reward systems of the brain are a group of structures that are activated whenever we experience something rewarding, such as eating a nice-tasting food, having sex, or using an addictive drug. When exposed to a stimulus that is rewarding, the brain responds by releasing an increased amount of dopamine, the main neurotransmitter associated with rewards and pleasure.'

'When the brain encounters a rewarding stimulus, whether it's an external object or an internal thought … this perception gets processed by various regions of the brain, including the hippocampus and the amygdala. Upon the recognition of the rewarding stimulus, the VTA [Ventral Tegmental Area] is stimulated to produce and release dopamine. Once dopamine is released from the VTA, it travels through the mesolimbic [or reward] pathway to the NAc [nucleus accumbens].' Here, 'dopamine binds to receptors on the surfaces of neurons, changing their activity. This change in neuronal activity is the underlying neurobiological event that translates to feelings of pleasure and reward'. Finally:

> 'As a result, the individual becomes more inclined to seek out or engage in that specific behavior or context in anticipation of the reward. Over time, through repeated exposures, this leads to learned behaviors or habits.'[1] So, every time Hardy, wittingly or unwittingly, relived his memories of Emma, his brain would have rewarded him in this way.

Clearly, Hardy's conscious mind would have recognized a photograph, electronic image, or portrait of Emma, as just that. But we may hypothesize, that his subconscious mind, or at any rate a part of it, interpreted the image as being the real, living person and stimulated the release of dopamine accordingly. Thus, a nightmarish situation, akin to an Alfred Hitchcock suspense and horror film, is initiated, whereby the helpless and hapless victim is conned into repeating the same futile action over and over again, obtaining nothing more than a fleeting, albeit pleasurable, reward from the dopamine 'kick', every time he or she reminds themselves of their deceased spouse. There is a distinct parallel between this and the type of addiction that a drug addict experiences, one difference being that dopamine is manufactured by the body itself.

Kvarnstrom agreed that 'In some ways, this cycle of reward-seeking is not unlike that experienced in addiction. Of course, this does not mean that complicated grief is intentional; the craving of neural rewards is an involuntary phenomenon that strips your loved one of the ability to move beyond a place of loss.' Florence knew only too well the extent to which Hardy was imprisoned by his grief.

Finally, 'risk factors that increase a person's likelihood of experiencing complicated bereavement', include 'unexpected death [as with Emma], such as death from an unknown illness [again, as with Emma] or accident, of a loved one'. This 'means that survivors have not had the opportunity to emotionally prepare for loss. Rather, survivors are thrown into loss suddenly and they may not have the inner resources to cope'.[2] Clearly, this was precisely the experience of Hardy, who declared that he was undone by the entire tragic experience of Emma's untimely death, viz his poem 'The Going':

> 'O you could not know
> That such swift fleeing
> No soul foreseeing
> Would undo me so'

The crucial question is, do the brain's Reward Systems *actually help* the CG sufferer? The answer is *a definite no!* All they have to offer is a temporary, dopamine-induced, feeling of pleasure. Are the Reward Systems of the brain actually *deleterious* to the CG sufferer? Yes, because they serve to lock the person into an obsessive habit of seeking reminders of the deceased partner over and over again, thus preventing him or her from seeking out genuine and lasting solace, companionship, compassion, empathy, love, and closure, in the real world.

Did Hardy, as seems highly likely, constantly remind himself of Emma by looking at photographs of her or at her portrait - after all, numerous photographs of her survived, as did her portrait? If so, it is as if the brain would have been unable to distinguish between images on celluloid or on canvas, from the former living Emma, and would therefore have triggered the release of dopamine in exactly the same way as if Hardy had encountered Emma in real life. In other words, it is as if the brain was playing tricks on Hardy's psyche, by locking him into an endless cycle of grief.

This, of course, has been the unfortunate experience of innumerable people throughout the world who have suffered bereavement, and it explains why a significant minority cannot escape from the symptoms and suffering caused by their 'Complicated Grief'.

Chapter 28

Aftermath

Hardy's collection of poems, entitled *Winter Words in Various Moods and Metres*, was published posthumously in 1928. On 9 December of that year, Hardy's brother Henry died aged 77.

In 1928, *The Early Life of Thomas Hardy 1840-1891* was published, with Florence as the author, but the text had undoubtedly been approved by Hardy.

On 11 July 1929 Florence wrote to Siegfried Sassoon to say:

> 'I do not think I shall take a house in London or make any change in my life. I feel that I belong to Max Gate where I can visit Stinsford & go to see my husband's sister (Kate] every few days.'[1]

In September 1929 Florence paid a visit to St Juliot, 'to the great pleasure of the solitary little clergyman who lives there' (the Reverend David Rhys Morris). However, despite the 'atmosphere of romance', Florence found the experience 'all very sad'.[2] In other words, Florence was depressed and still grieving for her late husband.

In 1930 *The Later Years of Thomas Hardy 1892-1928* was published, again with Florence as the author.

On 10 January 1931 Florence declared:

> 'With regard to the letters written by T.H. [Hardy] to E.L.G. - afterwards E.L.H. [Emma] - it was she who burnt his letters, & he told me he much regretted that at the time, & since. She asked him for her letters to him which he had carefully preserved, & she burnt those too.'[3] Surely this is an indication of Emma's intense animosity towards Hardy!

On 20 February 1932, four years after Hardy's death, Florence, in yet another eulogy to Hardy, wrote again to Harold Barlow, to say:

> 'It was such a wonderful thing to live in close association with that great mind & that noble personality. After having lived fourteen

> years with such a companion it is little wonder that I feel terribly lonely - & find the world very empty.'[4] Now it was Florence's turn to experience bereavement and all its horrors.

Florence continued to live at Max Gate until her death there on 15 October 1937, after a long illness. She was buried in Stinsford churchyard in the tomb of Hardy and his first wife, Emma. In her will she directed that Max Gate and its contents be sold at auction. In the event, Hardy's sister Kate purchased the property (even though she continued to live at Talbothays), and when she herself died in October 1940, aged 84, the property was left to the National Trust. (Hardy's boyhood home at Higher Bockhampton also now belongs to the National Trust.)

Chapter 29

Epilogue

Thomas Hardy, the son of his namesake Thomas, a Dorset mason and builder, and mother, Jemima, formerly a domestic servant, grew up to be a poet and novelist of such a distinction that the greatest literati of the day flocked to his door, and aristocratic households in his home county of Dorset and elsewhere were proud to open their doors to him.

On 7 March 1870, at St Juliot, Cornwall, Hardy met Emma Lavinia Gifford with whom he fell madly in love and, being a poet, versified rapturously about her! Both he and she were aged 29. Equally, in her book *Some Recollections*, Emma did likewise. But the mental disorders which afflicted several members of Emma's family came to afflict her, and to an ever-increasing degree. The outcome was that a schism developed between them which would never heal. Hardy was aged 72 when Emma died suddenly and unexpectedly 3 days after her 72nd birthday, whereupon he was overcome with grief and remorse.

Hardy was known to have neglected his wife in her later years, and although he told his friends that he did not blame Emma, who could not help her mental 'aberration' – to use his word - for the marital schism, in practice he came virtually to ignore her. This, he acknowledged after Emma's death, both in the poems and the letters which he wrote. For the remainder of his days, he harked back to the 'Emma as was', and especially to those rapturous, romantic days in Cornwall where he had courted her and which they had both enjoyed.

As a result of his neglect, Hardy's grief was tinged with guilt and remorse. Not only that, but in a sense, Hardy had been bereaved twice, having first 'lost' Emma all those years ago when her mental state deteriorated and she became mentally unstable, this in all probability being the principal reason why they became estranged. The love of his life had now become a stranger to him, and his feelings can scarcely be imagined! Precisely when this happened is not known, but his poems indicate that it was soon after their marriage. Finally, because Emma's death occurred so suddenly, there was no opportunity for reconciliation, apology, not even the chance to say 'goodbye', and Emma on her deathbed and unable to speak was the last memory Hardy would have had of her.

From the number of poems that Hardy wrote on the subject of religion it is clear that, whereas he would dearly have loved to embrace the Christian beliefs of his forebears, who looked forward to being reunited with their loved ones in heaven in the life hereafter, he was unable to do so. His reason told him that religion was invented by man out of fear, because it was impossible for men or women to believe that the spirits of those whom they had loved had simply vanished with their deaths. As T. S. Eliot said, 'I will show you fear in a handful of dust'.[1] And yet, Hardy envied those who *did* believe, and there were times, as already mentioned, when he *did* entertain the notion that there was an afterlife.

Hardy's poem *Heredity* was published in 1917:

> I am the family face;
> Flesh perishes, I live on,
> Projecting trait and trace
> Through time to times anon,
> And leaping from place to place
> Over oblivion.
>
> The years-heired feature that can
> In curve and voice and eye
> Despise the human span
> Of durance - that is I;
> The eternal thing in man,
> That heeds no call to die.

Heir: in this context meaning a person who inherits.

Here, there is no mention of 'God', or an 'Afterlife' – only 'oblivion' – the state of being unaware or unconscious of what is happening around one.[2] So perhaps, at the end of the day, Hardy believed that this was all that immortality consisted of – i.e. the continuation in successive generations of genetically inherited characteristics.

Hardy's grief and remorse are reflected in dozens of poems in which his relationship with Emma is thinly disguised – though he never mentioned her specifically by name. Furthermore, his novels and other writings deal with such themes as male/female relationships and marriage, and the virtual impossibility of a person escaping from 'holy wedlock' at that period of English history, even though the couple in question may find themselves to be completely incompatible.

How did Hardy survive the intense and prolonged grief which threatened to overwhelm him? The answer is, through the love and kindness of family and friends, and in particular, that of his second wife Florence, who was utterly devoted to him; by having Florence by his side, content in the knowledge that, as far as he was aware, she had liked Emma; by continuing to write poetry, especially about the late Emma, which was evidently a catharsis and a solace for him; revisiting St Juliot; by visiting Emma's birthplace and members of her family; and researching her family history. In addition, he visited her grave at Stinsford on appropriate anniversaries, and memorialized her with a commemorative plaque, placed in the church at St Juliot.

Given that, for Hardy, religions were invented phenomena, was there therefore, no prospect of immortality and an afterlife? Hardy saw 'God' as a force, or 'Will', that controls our destinies but is indifferent to our suffering. Ironically, his own lifetime experiences tend to bear this out! Nevertheless, although he renounced his Christian faith - he had once intended to become a vicar - he *did* hold out *some* hope that one day, he and Emma would be reunited.

Anyone who has lost a partner whom they had loved knows only too well, that the octopus-like tentacles of remembrance reach out constantly and unpredictably thereafter. Memories, some happy, some sad, and some deeply poignant, are rekindled whether we like it or not, often in the form of frightening flashbacks. One may imagine Hardy, for example, pondering over the fact that the last time he climbed the stairs at Max Gate, or strolled in the garden, or sat at his writing desk, or motored down a particular lane, or stroked her favourite cat; or heard the church bells ringing in the New Year, Emma was still alive; or saying to himself, 'Why am I still here? I did not ask for this! Why should I be condemned to go on without her?'

Of the two of them, with whom does one's sympathies lie? Certainly, with Emma, on account of the mental instability which ruined her life. But also with Hardy, who suffered in effect a 'double bereavement'. Was anyone to blame for them marrying? Certainly not Emma, who before long would be in the grip of a mental illness which was beyond her control, and into which she in all likelihood had little or no insight; and not Hardy, because Emma's symptoms had evidently not fully manifested themselves at the time of those early, heady days of courtship at St Juliot.

Is it fair to apportion blame either to Hardy or to Emma for their disastrous marriage? Probably not. Yes, Emma did exhibit appalling snobbishness towards Hardy right from the start but in this, she was undoubtedly influenced by her father John, who was equally snobbish. However, she subsequently despised, vilified, and denigrated Hardy over the course of many years. Why? Presumably because of her personality disorder, which is likely to have had its onset in her twenties and for which she was not responsible. And Hardy, for his part, not surprisingly reacted by largely cutting himself off from her.

What was the nature of Emma's mental disorder? She experienced grandiose and persecutory delusions, as a letter that she wrote to Hardy's sister Mary, a respectable and well thought of headteacher, indicates:

> 'You are a witch-like creature and quite equal to any amount of evil-wishing & speaking.'[3]

Mental disorders often occur throughout families, and this was certainly the case with Emma. Her niece Lilian Gifford experienced visual and auditory hallucinations and paranoia;[4] her eldest brother Richard Ireland Gifford experienced delusions and paranoia;[5] her father John Attersoll Gifford experienced auditory hallucinations and delusions.[6]

By the time of Emma's final illness, Hardy had become so numbed and disillusioned that he neglected her. He has been criticized for not seeking medical attention for her sooner but, to be fair, he was not fully aware of the seriousness of her condition, and Emma herself was loth to seek medical advice, perhaps because she was afraid of hospitals; after all, medical and surgical procedures tended to have a bad outcome in those times.

Today, Emma's gallstones would have been diagnosed, and she would have undergone a cholecystectomy (their surgical removal), which would have resolved the problem, whereupon she might have lived on for many years.

It is to his credit that Hardy acknowledged his neglect of Emma, and the remorse and torment which he suffered on this account for the remainder of his days is surely reflected in his subsequent poems and letters.

Some say that it is unfair to label Emma as having a personality disorder and may even go so far as to ignore or deny the evidence for it, even though that evidence is overwhelming. However, it is equally unfair to castigate Hardy, without recognising that he was a victim of his wife's personality disorder and had been for virtually the whole duration of their marriage.

The circumstances of Emma's death, and the background to it, bring to mind a song composed by US musician and singer Tom Paxton, entitled *The Last Thing on My Mind* (recorded by him and released on 1 January 1964):

> It's a lesson too late for the learnin'
> Made of sand, made of sand
> In the wink of an eye my soul is turnin'
> In your hand, in your hand
>
> Are you goin' away with no word of farewell?
> Will there be not a trace left behind?
> Well, I could have loved you better, didn't mean to be unkind
> You know that was the last thing on my mind
>
> Surely this was *exactly* how the bereaved Hardy must have felt and continued to feel, to his dying day!

The last words must be Hardy's, uttered vicariously by farmer Gabriel Oak, as he makes a proposal of marriage to Bathsheba Everdene, the beautiful young heroine, in Hardy's novel *Far from the Madding Crowd* (published in 1874). Having offered to buy her a piano, together with 'one of those little ten-pound gigs for market – and nice flowers – and birds – cocks and hens, I mean; and a frame for cucumbers', he declares that when they are married, 'and at home by the fire, whenever you look up, there shall I be – and whenever I look up, there will be you'.[7] Surely this is *precisely* what Hardy himself had longed for during his marriage to Emma. Sadly, it was not to be, and that was a tragedy for them both.

Notes

Chapter 1: Thomas Hardy: The First Seven Decades

1. A Timeline of Hardy's Life, up to the Death of Emma

1. Kate's birth entry, dated 2 September 1856, is in the name of 'Catherine'. Dorset Council Registration Services.
2. Flower, Newman, *Just as it Happened*, p.86.
3. 'William Barnes', *Wikipedia*.
4. Flower, op. cit., p.90.
5. Soanes, Catherine and Angus Stevenson (editors), *Oxford Dictionary of English*.
6. Hardy, Thomas, *The Hand of Ethelberta*, p.xiii.

2. Life Before Emma: How Hardy Pondered Over Life, Love, and Loss

1. Soanes, Catherine and Angus Stevenson (editors), *Oxford Dictionary of English*.

4. When Hardy Met Emma (7 March 1870)

1. Circular, issued from St Julitta's Rectory, March 1869.
2. Hardy, Evelyn and Robert Gittings (editors), *Some Recollections by Emma Hardy*, p.30.
3. Ibid, p.34.
4. Ibid, p.31.
5. 'Lyonesse', *Wikipedia*.

5. More About Emma

1. Hardy, Evelyn and Robert Gittings (editors), *Some Recollections by Emma Hardy*, p.30.
2. Memorial tablet in memory of Emma Gifford, designed by Hardy for the church of St Julitta, St Juliot, Cornwall, and erected in 1913.

6. Marital Discord

1. Hardy, Evelyn, *Thomas Hardy: A Critical Biography*, p.322.

2. Millgate, Michael (editor), *Letters of Emma and Florence Hardy*, Florence E. Dugdale to Edward Clodd, 7 March 1913.
3. Soanes, Catherine and Angus Stevenson (editors), *Oxford Dictionary of English*.
4. Ibid.
5. Ibid.

7. A Visit from the Prince of Wales: Dorchester Honours Hardy

1. Hardy, Florence, *The Life of Thomas Hardy,* Part II, *The Later Years of Thomas Hardy: 1892-1928*, p.143.
2. Ibid, p.143

Chapter 2: The Death of Emma (27 November 1912)

1. Hardy, Florence, *The Life of Thomas Hardy,* Part II, *The Later Years of Thomas Hardy: 1892-1928*, p.153.
2. Ibid, p.154.
3. Hardy, Florence, op. cit., p.154.
4. Ibid, p.156.
5. Ibid, p.154.
6. Weber, Carl J., *Hardy and the Lady from Madison Square*, p.165.

Chapter 3: Bereavement: The Contribution of Elisabeth Kübler-Ross and David Kessler

1. Kübler-Ross, Elisabeth and David Kessler, *On Grief and Grieving*, p.7.
2. Ibid, p.xi.

Chapter 4: Hardy and the Five Stages of Grief

1. Kübler-Ross, Elisabeth and David Kessler, *On Grief and Grieving*, p.8.
2. Soanes, Catherine and Angus Stevenson (editors), *Oxford Dictionary of English*.
3. Ibid.
4. Ibid.
5. Kübler-Ross, Elisabeth and David Kessler, op. cit., p.10.
6. Soanes, Catherine and Angus Stevenson (editors), op. cit.
7. Purdy, Richard Little and Michael Millgate, *The Collected Letters of Thomas Hardy*, Volume Four: Thomas Hardy to Edmund Gosse, 17 December 1912.
8. Ibid, to Lady Ilchester, 21 January 1913.

9. Kübler-Ross, Elisabeth and David Kessler, op. cit., p.11.
10. Ibid, p.13.
11. Ibid, p.15.
12. Ibid, p.17.
13. Ibid, p.17.
14. Ibid, pp.20-21.
15. Purdy, Richard Little and Michael Millgate, op. cit. Volume Four: Thomas Hardy to Florence Henniker, 17 December 1912.
16. Kübler-Ross, Elisabeth and David Kessler, op. cit., pp.24-5.
17. Soanes, Catherine and Angus Stevenson (editors), *Oxford Dictionary of English.*
18. Millgate, Michael (editor), *Letters of Emma and Florence Hardy*, Florence Dugdale to Edward Clodd, 21 August 1913.
19. Ibid, Florence Hardy to Rebekah Owen, 3 December 1915.

Chapter 5: Hardy and the Inner World of Grief

1. Kübler-Ross, Elisabeth and David Kessler, *On Grief and Grieving*, pp.29-30.
2. Soanes, Catherine and Angus Stevenson (editors), *Oxford Dictionary of English.*
3. Ibid.
4. Ibid.
5. Ibid.
6. Kübler-Ross, Elisabeth and David Kessler, op. cit., p.31.
7. Ibid, pp.33-4.
8. Ibid, p.38.
9. Purdy, Richard Little and Michael Millgate, *The Collected Letters of Thomas Hardy*, Volume Four: Thomas Hardy to Ellen Gosse, 12 December 1912.
10. Purdy, Richard Little and Michael Millgate, op. cit., Volume Five: Thomas Hardy to Florence Henniker, 17 July 1914.
11. Kübler-Ross, Elisabeth and David Kessler, op. cit., p.42
12. Purdy, Richard Little and Michael Millgate, op. cit., Volume Four: Thomas Hardy to George A. B. Dewar, 19 July 1917.
13. Soanes, Catherine and Angus Stevenson (editors), op. cit.
14. 'Angel of Death Name, Folklore and Symbolism', *WikiReligions.*
15. Soanes, Catherine and Angus Stevenson (editors), op. cit.
16. Ibid.
17. Ibid.
18. Kübler-Ross, Elisabeth and David Kessler, op. cit., p.48.
19. Soanes, Catherine and Angus Stevenson (editors), op. cit.
20. Ibid.

21. Kübler-Ross, Elisabeth and David Kessler, op. cit., p.52.
22. Ibid, p.54.
23. Soanes, Catherine and Angus Stevenson (editors), op. cit.
24. Ibid.
25. Ibid.
26. Kübler-Ross, Elisabeth and David Kessler, op. cit., p.58.
27. Ibid, pp.62-3.
28. Ibid, p.71.
29. Ibid, p.72.
30. Soanes, Catherine and Angus Stevenson (editors), op. cit.
31. Kübler-Ross, Elisabeth and David Kessler, op. cit., p.72.
32. Ibid, p.72.
33. Ibid, p.73.
34. Ibid, pp.80-1.
35. Soanes, Catherine and Angus Stevenson (editors), op. cit.
36. Ibid.
37. Ibid.
38. A quotation from the *Holy Bible*, New Testament, Book of Corinthians, 2: 5:4.
39. Hardy, Evelyn, *Thomas Hardy: A Critical Biography*, p.311.
40. Soanes, Catherine and Angus Stevenson (editors), op. cit.
41. Kübler-Ross, Elisabeth and David Kessler, op. cit., pp.81-2.
42. Ibid, p.83.
43. Ibid, p.87.
44. Flower, Newman, *Just as it Happened*, pp.95-6.
45. Hardy, Evelyn, op. cit., pp.276-7.
46. Kübler-Ross, Elisabeth and David Kessler, op. cit., p.89.
47. Ibid, p.95.
48. Ibid, p.98.
49. Soanes, Catherine and Angus Stevenson (editors), op. cit.
50. Ibid.
51. Kübler-Ross, Elisabeth and David Kessler, op. cit., p.102.
52. Ibid, p.108.
53. Soanes, Catherine and Angus Stevenson (editors), op. cit.
54. Ibid.
55. Ibid.

Chapter 6: Hardy and the Inner World of Grief: Hauntings

1. Soanes, Catherine and Angus Stevenson (editors), *Oxford Dictionary of English*.
2. Kübler-Ross, Elisabeth and David Kessler, *On Grief and Grieving*, pp.55-6.

3. Soanes, Catherine and Angus Stevenson (editors), op. cit.
4. Ibid.
5. Ibid.
6. Merriam-Webster Dictionary online.

Chapter 7:Thomas Hardy and the Outer World of Grief

1. Kübler-Ross, Elisabeth and David Kessler, *On Grief and Grieving*, p.115.
2. Hardy, Florence, *The Life of Thomas Hardy,* Part II, *The Later Years of Thomas Hardy: 1892-1928*, p.229.
3. Ibid, p.237.
4. Kübler-Ross, Elisabeth and David Kessler, op. cit., pp.120–1.
5. Ibid, p.126.
6. Soanes, Catherine and Angus Stevenson (editors), *Oxford Dictionary of English.*
7. Kübler-Ross, Elisabeth and David Kessler, op. cit., p.129.
8. Flower, Newman, *Just as it Happened*, p.96.
9. Kübler-Ross, Elisabeth and David Kessler, op. cit., p.133.
10. Gittings, Robert, *The Older Hardy*, p.151.
11. Soanes, Catherine and Angus Stevenson (editors), op. cit. The two copies of *Spaces* were auctioned in the USA after the contents of Max Gate were sold in 1938. William P. Wreden, Burlingame, California: 'A Selection of Books from the Library of Thomas Hardy, O.M.' 'Hardy (Emma L.) Lot 163. *Spaces*. Max Gate 1912. Fine Copy', and a second 'Fine Copy' with 'Mrs Hardy's personal card inserted'. 'Catalogue No.11, 1938'. Dorset History Centre, DHC H. 1983-400. Sanders 4.9.
12. Kübler-Ross, Elisabeth and David Kessler, op. cit., p.137.
13. Ibid, p.143.
14. Ibid, p.144.
15. Soanes, Catherine and Angus Stevenson (editors), op. cit.
16. Kübler-Ross, Elisabeth and David Kessler, op. cit., p.153.
17. Ibid, p.154.
18. Ibid, p.158.
19. 'Coping with Flashbacks during Bereavement', NHS, MindWell.

Chapter 8: When Death is Sudden and Unexpected

1. Kübler-Ross, Elisabeth and David Kessler, *On Grief and Grieving*, p.195.
2. Ibid, pp.195-6.
3. Ibid, p.198.

4. Ibid, p.209.
5. Purdy, Richard Little and Michael Millgate, *The Collected Letters of Thomas Hardy*, Volume Four: Thomas Hardy to Charles Edwin Gifford, 27 November 1912.
6. Purdy, Richard Little and Michael Millgate, *The Collected Letters of Thomas Hardy*, Volume Four: Thomas Hardy to the Reverend Alfred Metcalfe, 29 November 1912.
7. Ibid, Volume Four: Thomas Hardy to Florence Henniker, 17 December 1912.
8. Ibid, Volume Four: Thomas Hardy to Lady Agnes Grove, 21 December 1912.
9. Ibid, Volume Four: Thomas Hardy to Sir Robert Pearce Edgcumbe, 26 December 1912.

Chapter 9: Thomas Hardy's Personal Experience of Bereavement

1. Purdy, Richard Little and Michael Millgate, *The Collected Letters of Thomas Hardy*, Volume Five: Thomas Hardy to Florence Henniker, 28 December 1918.
2. Ibid, Volume Four: Thomas Hardy to Edward Clodd, 3 December 1912.
3. Hardy, Florence, *The Life of Thomas Hardy,* Part II, *The Later Years of Thomas Hardy: 1892-1928*, p.156.
4. Soanes, Catherine and Angus Stevenson (editors), *Oxford Dictionary of English*.
5. Ibid.
6. Ibid.
7. Ibid.
8. Ibid.
9. Ibid.
10. Ibid.
11. Ibid.

Chapter 10: Hardy's Feelings of Guilt over his Treatment of Emma

1. Pinion, F. B., *Thomas Hardy: His Life and Friends*, Pinion, p.315.
2. Flower, Newman, *Just as it Happened*, pp.95-6.
3. Soanes, Catherine and Angus Stevenson (editors), *Oxford Dictionary of English*.

4. Ibid.
5. Purdy, Richard Little and Michael Millgate, *The Collected Letters of Thomas Hardy*, Volume Four: Thomas Hardy to Florence Henniker, 17 December 1912.
6. Millgate, Michael (editor), *Letters of Emma and Florence Hardy*, Florence E. Dugdale to Edward Clodd, 20 April 1913.
7. Soanes, Catherine and Angus Stevenson (editors), op. cit.
8. Purdy, Richard Little and Michael Millgate, op. cit., Volume 5: Thomas Hardy to Sydney Cockerell, 26 April 1916.

Chapter 11: Did Hardy and Emma Have Anything in Common at all?

1. Soanes, Catherine and Angus Stevenson (editors), *Oxford Dictionary of English.*
2. Hardy, Thomas, *Far from the Madding Crowd*, Chapter 51.
3. Purdy, Richard Little and Michael Millgate, *The Collected Letters of Thomas Hardy*, Volume Four: Thomas Hardy to Florence Henniker, 17 December 1912.
4. 1904, Thomas Hardy interview with literary critic William Archer, in F. B. Pinion, *A Hardy Companion*, p.178.
5. Soanes, Catherine and Angus Stevenson (editors), op. cit.
6. Hardy, Florence, *The Life of Thomas Hardy,* Part II, *The Later Years of Thomas Hardy: 1892-1928*, p.251.
7. Hardy, Evelyn, *Thomas Hardy: A Critical Biography*, p.270.

Chapter 12: Emma's Mental State

1. Hardy and Others were Aware that Emma was Mentally Unstable

1. Purdy, Richard Little and Michael Millgate, *The Collected Letters of Thomas Hardy*, Volume Five: Thomas Hardy to the Reverend J. H. Dickinson, 16 February 1914.
2. Ibid, Volume Five: Thomas Hardy to Florence Henniker, 6 March 1914.
3. Ibid, Volume Five: Thomas Hardy to Kate Gifford, 23 November 1914.
4. Soanes, Catherine and Angus Stevenson (editors), *Oxford Dictionary of English.*
5. Stevens Cox, J., *Thomas Hardy: Materials for a Study of his Life, Times, and Works*, Monograph No.18.
6. Stevens Cox, J., op. cit., Monogram No.14.
7. Dr F. B. Fisher to Lady Hoare, 25 January 1928, Wiltshire Record Office.

8. Stevens Cox, J., op. cit., Monogram No.16.
9. Ibid, Monogram No.16.
10. Soanes, Catherine and Angus Stevenson (editors), op. cit.
11. A. C. Benson, *Diary*, 5 September 1912, Magdalene College, Cambridge.
12. Purdy, Richard Little and Michael Millgate, op. cit., Volume Four: Thomas Hardy to Florence Henniker, 17 December 1912.
13. Clodd, Edward, *Diary* (unpublished), 13 July 1913, quoted in Denys Kay-Robinson, *The First Mrs Thomas Hardy*, p.257.
14. Kate Gifford to Thomas Hardy, 25 November 1914, Dorset County Museum.
15. See Norman, Andrew, *Thomas Hardy: Behind the Mask*.
16. Hardy, Evelyn and Robert Gittings (editors), *Some Recollections by Emma Hardy*, p.35.
17. *Holy Bible*, Old Testament Book of Daniel, Chapter 3, Verses 8-30.
18. Collins, Vere H., *Talks with Thomas Hardy at Max Gate*, p.25.
19. Hardy, Evelyn, *Thomas Hardy: A Critical Biography*, pp.272-3.
20. Soanes, Catherine and Angus Stevenson (editors), op. cit.
21. Hardy, Evelyn, op. cit., p.273.
22. Ibid, p.273.

2. Emma's Religious Mania

1. Flower, Newman, *Just as it Happened*, p.95.
2. Hardy E. and F. B. Pinion (editors), *One Rare Fair Woman: Thomas Hardy's Letters to Florence Henniker, 1893-1922*, p.154.
3. Hunter, Richard and Ida Macalpine, *Psychiatry for the Poor*.
4. Gittings, Robert, *The Older Hardy*, p.151.
5. Hardy, Evelyn, *Thomas Hardy: A Critical Biography*, pp.269-70.

Chapter 14: Did Hardy Ever Regret Having Married Emma?

1. *Jude the Obscure*, Preface.
2. The Matrimonial Causes Act, 1857, *Wikipedia*.
3. Hardy, Thomas, *Jude the Obscure*, p.220.
4. Guo, Yu-hua, 'On Hardy's View on Marriage Through the Marriage of Sue and Phillotson', US-China Foreign Language, August 2017, Vol. 15, No. 8, pp. 510-515, doi:10.17265/1539-8080/2017.08.005, Binzhou University, Binzhou, Chin.
5. Soanes, Catherine and Angus Stevenson (editors), *Oxford Dictionary of English*.

Chapter 15: Despite all, Hardy, in Retrospect, Strove to See Emma in the Best Possible Light

1. Purdy, Richard Little and Michael Millgate, *The Collected Letters of Thomas Hardy*, Volume Four: Thomas Hardy to Florence Dugdale, 29 January 1913.
2. Soanes, Catherine and Angus Stevenson (editors), *Oxford Dictionary of English.*
3. Flower, Newman, *Just as it Happened*, p.95.

Chapter 16: The Important Testimony of Alice ('Dolly') Gale

1. Baigent, Beryl, '80 Years Ago in the Thomas Hardy Household', *The Thomas Hardy Journal*, 8.3 (October 1992), pp.69-75. Information kindly supplied by Dr Tracy Hayes, Secretary; Website & Social Media Director, The Thomas Hardy Society.
2. Cox, J. Stevens, 'I was Emma Lavinia's Personal Maid', *The Thomas Hardy Year Book*, 4 (1974), pp.6-9. Information kindly supplied by Dr Tracy Hayes, Secretary; Website & Social Media Director, The Thomas Hardy Society.
3. Baigent, Beryl, op. cit., pp.69-75.
4. Cox, J. Stevens, op. cit., pp.6-9.
5. See Norman, Andrew, *Thomas Hardy: Bockhampton and Beyond.*
6. Cox, J. Stevens, op. cit., pp.6-9.
7. Soanes, Catherine and Angus Stevenson (editors), *Oxford Dictionary of English.*
8. Baigent, Beryl, op. cit., pp.69-75.
9. Cox, J. Stevens, op. cit., pp.6-9.
10. Baigent, Beryl, op. cit., pp.69-75.
11. Cox, J. Stevens, op. cit., pp.6-9.
12. Baigent, Beryl, op. cit., pp.69-75.
13. Cox, J. Stevens, op. cit., pp.6-9.
14. Baigent, Beryl, op. cit., pp.69-75.
15. Cox, J. Stevens, op. cit., pp.6-9.
16. Baigent, Beryl, op. cit., pp.69-75.
17. Cox, J. Stevens, op. cit., pp.6-9.
18. Baigent, Beryl, op. cit., pp.69-75.
19. Ibid, pp.69-75.
20. 'I Was Emma Lavinia's Personal Maid by Alice Harvey ('Dolly Gale'), *The Thomas Hardy Year Book*, 4 (1974), pp.6-9.

Chapter 16: Hardy's Neglect of Emma

1. Hardy, Florence, *The Life of Thomas Hardy,* Part II, *The Later Years of Thomas Hardy: 1892-1928*, p.154.

Chapter 18: Hardy and Time; the Afterlife; Einstein

1. Hardy's Preoccupation with Time

1. Hardy, Florence, *The Life of Thomas Hardy,* Part I, *The Early Life of Thomas Hardy 1840-1891*, p.265.
2. Soanes, Catherine and Angus Stevenson (editors), *Oxford Dictionary of English.*
3. Ferguson, Trish (editor), *Literature and Modern Time*: '"Time's Renewal": Death and Immortality in Thomas Hardy's "Emma Poems"'.
4. Hardy, Thomas, *Tess of the d'Urbervilles*, Chapter 58.
5. Ferguson, Trish, op. cit., p.150.
6. Soanes, Catherine and Angus Stevenson (editors), op. cit.
7. Ibid.
8. Ibid.
9. Ibid.
10. Cronin, Richard (editor), *A Companion to Victorian Poetry*, Seamus Perry, 'Elegy'.
11. Ferguson, Trish, op. cit., p.151.
12. Soanes, Catherine and Angus Stevenson (editors), op. cit.
13. Ibid.
14. Ibid.
15. Ibid.
16. Ibid.
17. Ibid.
18. Ibid.
19. Ibid.
20. Soanes, Catherine and Angus Stevenson (editors), op. cit.
21. Ibid.

2. Hardy, Emma, and the 'Afterlife'

1. *Pall Mall Magazine*, April 1901.
2. Soanes, Catherine and Angus Stevenson (editors), *Oxford Dictionary of English.*
3. Ibid.
4. Merriam-Webster Dictionary online.

5. Ferguson, Trish (editor), *Literature and Modern Time*: '"Time's Renewal": Death and Immortality in Thomas Hardy's "Emma Poems"', p.166.
6. Soanes, Catherine and Angus Stevenson (editors), op. cit.
7. Ibid.

3. Albert Einstein: for Hardy, the Answer to a Prayer?

1. Soanes, Catherine and Angus Stevenson (editors), *Oxford Dictionary of English.*
2. Einstein: *Relativity: The Special and the General Theory: A Popular Exposition*, Third Edition (Methuen, London, 1920).
3. Millgate, Michael (editor), *Letters of Emma and Florence Hardy,* Florence Hardy to Alda, Lady Hoare, 21 June 1921.
4. Purdy, Richard Little and Michael Millgate, *The Collected Letters of Thomas Hardy*, Volume Five: Thomas Hardy to J. M. E. McTaggart, 31 December 1919.
5. Taylor, Richard H., *The Personal Notebooks of Thomas Hardy*, p.71.
6. Ferguson, Trish (editor), *Literature and Modern Time*: '"Time's Renewal": Death and Immortality in Thomas Hardy's "Emma Poems"', p.167.
7. Soanes, Catherine and Angus Stevenson (editors), op. cit.
8. Merriam-Webster Dictionary online.
9. Merriam-Webster Dictionary online.
10. Soanes, Catherine and Angus Stevenson (editors), op. cit.
11. Ibid.
12. Ibid.
13. Ibid.
14. Ibid.
15. Ibid.
16. Ibid.
17. Ibid.

4. Einstein and Michele Besso

1. 'Lieber Vero und liebe Frau Bice', Princeton, 21 March 1955. Christie's auctioneers, London: Live Auction 14299, 'Valuable Books and Manuscripts', closed 12 July 2017.
2. Soanes, Catherine and Angus Stevenson (editors), *Oxford Dictionary of English.*
3. Einstein, Albert, *Relativity: The Special and the General Theory: A Popular Exposition*, p.91.
4. Soanes, Catherine and Angus Stevenson (editors), op. cit.
5. Ibid.
6. Einstein, Albert, op. cit., p.91.

5. Einstein: Hardy's Huge Misinterpretation

1. Dukas, Helen and Banesh Hoffman (editors), *Albert Einstein: The Human Side*, Albert Einstein, statement, 5 February 1921, attributed in posthumous publications, letter of February 5, 1921, p.40.
2. Soanes, Catherine and Angus Stevenson (editors), *Oxford Dictionary of English*.
3. Einstein, Albert: *The World as I See It*, p.5.
4. Dukas, Helen and Banesh Hoffman (editors), op. cit., Albert Einstein, reply to a letter sent to him on 17 July 1953, attributed in posthumous publications, p.39.

6. Hardy's Final Days: Four Important Poems

1. Hardy, Florence, *The Life of Thomas Hardy,* Part II, *The Later Years of Thomas Hardy: 1892-1928*, p.264.
2. Soanes, Catherine and Angus Stevenson (editors), *Oxford Dictionary of English*.
3. Hardy, Florence, op. cit., p.265.
4. Ibid, p.265.
5. Alam, Dr Ejaz, Associate Professor and Head of English at Maulana Mazharul Haque Arabic and Persian University, Patna, Bihar, India: CC-6 (Sem-2), 'Critical Analysis of Rabbi Ben Ezra', online.
6. Hardy, Florence, op. cit., p.266.

Chapter 19: Hardy's Later Years

1. Further Honours for Hardy

1. The 'Poets' Tribute' book, compiled and presented to Hardy in 1919 on his 79th birthday by Siegfried Sassoon.
2. Hardy, Florence, *The Life of Thomas Hardy,* Part II, *The Later Years of Thomas Hardy: 1892-1928*, p.234.

2. Marriage to Florence Dugdale (10 February 1914)

1. Letter from Florence Hardy to Harold Barlow, 24 February 1914. Dorset History Centre.
2. Hardy, Florence, *The Life of Thomas Hardy,* Part II, *The Later Years of Thomas Hardy: 1892-1928*, p.172.
3. Ibid, p.173.
4. Millgate, Michael (editor), *Letters of Emma and Florence Hardy,* Florence Hardy to Sydney Cockerell, 1 September 1916.
5. Hardy, Florence, op. cit., 225-6.

3. What Florence had Really Thought of Emma

1. Millgate, Michael (editor), *Letters of Emma and Florence Hardy*, Florence E. Dugdale to Edward Clodd, 16 January 1913.
2. Ibid, Florence Dugdale to Edward Clodd, 30 January 1913.
3. Ibid, Florence E. Dugdale to Edward Clodd, 7 March 1913.
4. Ibid, Florence Dugdale to Edward Clodd, 11 March 1913.
5. Pinion, F. B., *Thomas Hardy: His Life and Friends*, p.237.
6. Millgate, Michael (editor), op. cit., Florence Hardy to Rebekah Owen, 18 January 1916.
7. Purdy, Richard Little and Michael Millgate, *The Collected Letters of Thomas Hardy*, Volume Five: Thomas Hardy to the Reverend J. H. Dickinson, 6 September 1916.
8. Ibid, Volume Six: Thomas Hardy to Reverend J. H. Dickinson, 15 June 1920.
9. Hardy, Evelyn, *Thomas Hardy: A Critical Biography*, p.119.
10. Florence Hardy to Vere Collins, privately printed note to *The Love Poetry of Thomas Hardy*, in Evelyn, p.119.

4. The Death of Hardy's Sister Mary

1. Hardy, Florence, *The Life of Thomas Hardy,* Part II, *The Later Years of Thomas Hardy: 1892-1928*, p.170.

7. Hardy's Incivility and Meanness

1. Hardy, Florence, *The Life of Thomas Hardy,* Part I, *The Early Life of Thomas Hardy 1840-1891*, p.294.
2. Soanes, Catherine and Angus Stevenson (editors), *Oxford Dictionary of English.*
3. Cox, J. Stevens, *Thomas Hardy: Materials for a Study of his Life, Times, and Works*, Monogram Numbers 5,6,7,14.

8. Was Hardy a Pessimist?

1. Soanes, Catherine and Angus Stevenson (editors), *Oxford Dictionary of English.*
2. Ibid.
3. Thomas Hardy, conversation with William Archer, 1904, in F. B. Pinion, *A Hardy Companion*, p.178.
4. Flower, Newman, *Just as it Happened*, p.94.
5. Hardy, Florence, *The Life of Thomas Hardy,* Part II, *The Later Years of Thomas Hardy: 1892-1928*, p.245.
6. Francis Edwards Ltd, Booksellers, London, Catalogue No. 1023. 1979. Item No. 284. Siegfried Sassoon to Philip E. Morell, 20 September 1956. Dorset History Centre: Saunders 4.9. H8066.
7. Soanes, Catherine and Angus Stevenson (editors), op. cit.

9. Hardy and Persistent Complex Bereavement Disorder

1. *Diagnostic and Statistical Manual of Mental Disorders, Fifth Edition,* pp.790-1.
2. 'Psychosocial', *Wikipedia.*

10. How Hardy Cherished the Memory of Lost Loved Ones

1. Merriam-Webster Dictionary online.
2. Soanes, Catherine and Angus Stevenson (editors), *Oxford Dictionary of English.*

11. Hardy as a Subject for Psychological Study!

1. Millgate, Michael (editor), *Letters of Emma and Florence Hardy*, Florence E. Dugdale to Edward Clodd, 20 April 1913.

Chapter 20: Further Likely Reasons for Emma's Dislike of Hardy

1. Millgate, Michael (editor), *Letters of Emma and Florence Hardy*, Emma Hardy to Elspeth Grahame, 20 August 1899.
2. Taylor, Richard H., *Emma Hardy Diaries*, p.32.

Chapter 21: Did Emma *Ever* Love Hardy?

1. Hardy, Evelyn and Robert Gittings (editors), *Some Recollections by Emma Hardy*, pp.xiii-xiv.
2. Ibid, pp.30-1.
3. Ibid, pp.33-4.
4. Ibid, p.35.
5. Ibid, p.37.

Chapter 22: How did Hardy Survive the Loss of Emma? his Coping Mechanisms

1. How the Mind Deals with Memories

1. Kübler-Ross, Elisabeth and David Kessler, *On Grief and Grieving*, p.61.
2. Ibid, p.119.

2. How Distractions Offered Hardy a Diversion from Painful Memories

1. Purdy, Richard Little and Michael Millgate, *The Collected Letters of Thomas Hardy*, Volume Four: Thomas Hardy to Lady Ilchester, 21 January 1913.

4. How Hardy Came to Depend on Florence: Mutual Support.

1. Flower, Newman, *Just as it Happened*, p.96.
2. Purdy, Richard Little and Michael Millgate, *The Collected Letters of Thomas Hardy*, Volume Four: Thomas Hardy to Florence E. Hardy, 29 January 1913.
3. Ibid, Volume Five: Thomas Hardy to Florence Henniker, 17 July 1914.
4. Millgate, Michael (editor), *Letters of Emma and Florence Hardy*, Florence E. Hardy to Lady Hoare, 9 December 1914.

5. Hardy's Memorial to Emma

1. Purdy, Richard Little and Michael Millgate, *The Collected Letters of Thomas Hardy*, Volume Four: Thomas Hardy to the Reverend J. H. Dickinson, 1 June 1913.
2. Ibid, Volume Five: Thomas Hardy to John Galsworthy, 16 April 1916.
3. Hardy, Florence, *The Life of Thomas Hardy,* Part I, *The Early Life of Thomas Hardy 1840-1891*, p.90.
4. Purdy, Richard Little and Michael Millgate, op. cit., Volume Five: Thomas Hardy to Florence Henniker, 4 September 1916.

6. A Continuity of Lifestyle

1. Purdy, Richard Little and Michael Millgate, *The Collected Letters of Thomas Hardy*, Volume Five: Thomas Hardy to the Reverend J. H. Dickinson, 16 February 1914.
2. Ibid, Volume Five: Thomas Hardy to A. C. Benson, 2 March 1914.
3. Ibid, Volume Five: Thomas Hardy to Frederic Harrison, 17 February 1914.

7. Did Hardy Find Any Solace in Religion?

1. Blaxland, Beth and Fran Dorey, 'Sharing a Common Ancestor: Early Ancestors', Australian Museum online, 2 November 2018.
2. Soanes, Catherine and Angus Stevenson (editors), op. cit.
3. Ibid.
4. Ibid.
5. Ibid.
6. Ibid.
7. Ibid.
8. Merriam-Webster Dictionary online.
9. Soanes, Catherine and Angus Stevenson (editors), op. cit.
10. Ibid.
11. Ibid.
12. Welford, John, 'Great Poetry Explained': 'A Plaint to Man' by Thomas Hardy', 31 December 2018, online.

Chapter 24: How Hardy Mourned his Loss of Faith

1. Hardy, Evelyn, *Thomas Hardy: A Critical Biography*, p.141.
2. Soanes, Catherine and Angus Stevenson (editors), *Oxford Dictionary of English*.
3. Ibid.
4. Ibid.
5. Ibid.
6. Welford, John, 'Great Poetry Explained': 'God's Funeral, by Thomas Hardy', 16 January 2019 online.
7. Hardy, Florence, *The Life of Thomas Hardy,* Part II, *The Later Years of Thomas Hardy: 1892-1928*, p.176.

Chapter 25: Proof of Hardy's Recovery, Albeit Fragile!

1. Millgate, Michael (editor), *Letters of Emma and Florence Hardy*, Florence E. Dugdale to Edward Clodd, 7 March 1913.
2. Ibid, Florence E. Dugdale to Edward Clodd, 20 April 1913.
3. Ibid, Florence E. Dugdale to Edward Clodd, 21 August 1913.

Chapter 26: The Death of Hardy (11 January 1928)

1. Flower, Newman, *Just as it Happenned*, p.99.
2. Dean of Westminster to the Reverend Richard G. Bartlett, Vicar of St George's Church, Fordington, 16 January 1928. Dorset History Centre.

Chapter 27: Science Sheds New Light on 'Complicated Grief'

1. Guy-Evans, Olivia, 'Brain Reward System', *Simply Psychology*, 14 September 2023 online.
2. Kvarnstrom, Elisabet, 'How to Help Someone with Complicated Bereavement: Fostering Understanding and Seeking Treatment', *Bridges to Recovery* online, 4 January 2018.

Chapter 28: Aftermath

1. Millgate, Michael (editor), *Letters of Emma and Florence Hardy*, Florence Hardy to Siegfried Sassoon, 11 July 1929.

2. Ibid, Florence Hardy to Howard Bliss, 29 September 1929.
3. Ibid, Florence Hardy to Howard Bliss, 10 January 1931.
4. Florence Hardy to Harold Barlow, 20 February 1932. Dorset History Centre.

Chapter 29: Epilogue

1. T. S. Eliot, poem *The Waste Land*, published 1922.
2. Soanes, Catherine and Angus Stevenson (editors), *Oxford Dictionary of English*.
3. Letters of E and F pp.7-8.
4. 'Order for Reception of a Pauper Lunatic' (Ethel Lilian Attersoll Gifford), signed 25 July 1919 to Claybury Asylum, Essex. The original copy of the order was destroyed but Professor Millgate had previously obtained a copy, and he kindly made it available to the author. Information kindly supplied by Warneford Hospital, Oxford, Case Books WV 154 vi-viii and Reception Papers WV 169 i.
5. 'Order for Reception of a Pauper Lunatic', op. cit.
6. 'Order for Reception of a Pauper Lunatic', op. cit. Doc. HC/1/45/19, Cornwall Records Office.
7. Hardy, Thomas, *Far from the Madding Crowd*, p.33.

Bibliography

Baigent, Beryl, '80 Years Ago in the Thomas Hardy Household', *The Thomas Hardy Journal*, 8.3 (October 1992), pp.69-75. Information kindly supplied by Dr Tracy Hayes, Secretary; Website & Social Media Director, The Thomas Hardy Society.

Collins, Vere H., *Talks with Thomas Hardy at Max Gate* (Duckworth, London, 1978).

Cox, J. Stevens, 'I was Emma Lavinia's Personal Maid', *The Thomas Hardy Year Book*, 4 (1974), pp.6-9. Information kindly supplied by Dr Tracy Hayes, Secretary; Website & Social Media Director, The Thomas Hardy Society.

Cronin, Richard (editor), *A Companion to Victorian Poetry*, (Blackwell, Oxford, UK, 2007).

Diagnostic and Statistical Manual of Mental Disorders, Fifth Edition, DSM-5th (American Psychiatric Association, Washington DC and London, 2013).

Dukas, Helen and Banesh Hoffman (editors), *Albert Einstein: The Human Side* (Princeton University Press, Princeton, NJ, 1979).

Einstein, Albert: *The World as I See It* (Citadel Press, Secaucus, NJ, 1999).

Einstein: *Relativity: The Special and the General Theory: A Popular Exposition*, Third Edition (Methuen, London, 1920).

Ferguson, Trish (editor), *Literature and Modern Time* (Springer Nature, Switzerland, 2020).

Flower, Newman, *Just as it Happenned* (Cassell, London, 1950).

Gittings, Robert, *The Older Hardy* (Heinemann, London, 1978).

Hardy E. and F. B. Pinion (editors), *One Rare Fair Woman: Thomas Hardy's Letters to Florence Henniker, 1893-1922* (Macmillan, London, 1972),

Hardy, Evelyn, *Thomas Hardy: A Critical Biography* (The Hogarth Press, London, 1954).

Hardy, Evelyn and Robert Gittings (editors), *Some Recollections by Emma Hardy* (Oxford University Press, Oxford, UK, 1979).

Hardy, Florence, *The Life of Thomas Hardy,* Part I, *The Early Life of Thomas Hardy 1840-1891*. Part II, *The Later Years of Thomas Hardy: 1892-1928* (Studio Editions, London, 1994).

Hardy, Thomas, *Far from the Madding Crowd* (Marshall Cavendish Partworks, London, 1991).

Hardy, Thomas, *The Hand of Ethelberta* (*Penguin Books*, London, 1997).

Hardy, Thomas, *Jude the Obscure* (Macmillan, London, 1974).

Hunter, Richard and Ida Macalpine, *Psychiatry for the Poor* (Dawsons, Pall Mall, London, 1851).

Kay-Robinson, Denys, *The First Mrs Thomas Hardy* (Macmillan, London, 1979).

Kübler-Ross, Elisabeth, *On Death and Dying* (Routledge, London, 1969).

Kübler-Ross, Elisabeth and David Kessler, *On Grief and Grieving* (Simon & Schuster, New York, 2005).

Larkin, Philip, *The Poetry of Hardy* (Faber & Faber, London, 1983).

Merriam-Webster Dictionary online.

Millgate, Michael (editor), Letters of Emma and Florence Hardy (Clarendon Press, Oxford, UK, 1996).

Millgate, Michael and Keith Wilson, *The Collected Letters of Thomas Hardy*, Volume Eight, 1861-1927 (Oxford University Press, Oxford, UK, 1985).

Norman, Andrew, *Thomas Hardy: Behind the Mask* (The History Press, Stroud, UK, 2011).

Norman, Andrew, *Thomas Hardy: Bockhampton and Beyond* (Halsgrove, Wellington, Somerset, UK, 2017).

Pinion, F. B., *Thomas Hardy: His Life and Friends* (Macmillan, London, 1994).

Purdy, Richard Little and Michael Millgate, *The Collected Letters of Thomas Hardy*, Volume Four, 1909-1913 (Clarendon Press, Oxford, UK, 1984).

Purdy, Richard Little and Michael Millgate, *The Collected Letters of Thomas Hardy*, Volume Five, 1914-1919 (Oxford University Press, Oxford, UK, 1985).

Purdy, Richard Little and Michael Millgate, *The Collected Letters of Thomas Hardy*, Volume Six, 1920-1925 (Oxford University Press, Oxford, UK, 1985).

Soanes, Catherine and Angus Stevenson (editors), *Oxford Dictionary of English* (Oxford University Press, Oxford, New York, 2005).

Stevens Cox, J., *Thomas Hardy: Materials for a Study of his Life, Times, and Works* (Toucan Press, Guernsey, UK, 1964).

Taylor, Richard H., *Emma Hardy Diaries* (Mid-Northumberland Arts Group and *Carcanet New Press*, 1985).

Taylor, Richard H., *The Personal Notebooks of Thomas Hardy* (Macmillan, London, 1979).

Weber, Carl J., *Hardy and the Lady from Madison Square* (Colby College Press, Maine, USA, 1952).

By the Same Author

By Swords Divided: Corfe Castle in the Civil War. Halsgrove, 2003.
Thomas Hardy: Christmas Carollings. Halsgrove, 2005.
Enid Blyton and her Enchantment with Dorset. Halsgrove, 2005.
Tyneham: A Tribute. Halsgrove, 2007.
Agatha Christie: The Finished Portrait. Tempus, 2007.
The Story of George Loveless and the Tolpuddle Martyrs. Halsgrove, 2008.
Father of the Blind: A Portrait of Sir Arthur Pearson. The History Press, 2009.
Agatha Christie: The Pitkin Guide. Pitkin Publishing, 2009.
Arthur Conan Doyle: The Man behind Sherlock Holmes. The History Press, 2009.
HMS Hood: Pride of the Royal Navy. The History Press, 2009.
Purbeck Personalities. Halsgrove, 2009.
Bournemouth's Founders and Famous Visitors. The History Press, 2010.
Thomas Hardy: Behind the Mask. The History Press, 2011.
A Brummie Boy goes to War. Halsgrove, 2011.
Winston Churchill: Portrait of an Unquiet Mind. Pen & Sword Books, 2012.
Charles Darwin: Destroyer of Myths. Pen & Sword Books, 2013.
Beatrix Potter: Her Inner World. Pen & Sword Books, 2013.
T.E. Lawrence: Tormented Hero. Fonthill, 2014.
Agatha Christie: The Disappearing Novelist. Fonthill, 2014.
Lawrence of Arabia's Clouds Hill. Halsgrove, 2014.
Jane Austen: Love is Like a Rose. Fonthill, 2015.
Kindly Light: The Story of Blind Veterans UK. Fonthill, 2015.
Thomas Hardy at Max Gate: The Latter Years. Halsgrove, 2016.
Corfe Remembered. Halsgrove, 2017.
Thomas Hardy: Bockhampton and Beyond. Halsgrove, 2017.
Mugabe: Monarch of Blood and Tears. Austin Macauley, 2017
Making Sense of Marilyn. Fonthill, 2018.
Hitler's Insanity: A Conspiracy of Silence. Fonthill, 2018.
The Unwitting Fundamentalist. Austin Macauley, 2018.
Robert Mugabe's Lost Jewel of Africa. Fonthill, 2018.
Hitler: Dictator or Puppet? Pen & Sword, 2011, 2020.

By the Same Author

Halsewell: A Shipwreck that Gripped the Nation. Fonthill, 2020.
The Amazing Story of Lise Meitner. Pen & Sword, 2021.
Paul Robeson: A Song For Freedom. New Haven Publishing, 2022
Francoise Hardy: A Musical Tale of Love and Loss. New Haven Publishing, 2022.
The Real Sir Arthur Conan Doyle. Pen & Sword, 2023.
A Dorset Childhood: Growing up in the Land of the Tolpuddle Martyrs at the Time of the Cold War. Pen & Sword, 2023.
A Purbeck Romance: Set in Thomas Hardy's Glorious Wessex. Pen & Sword, 2023.

Index